美丽的
The Charms of China

中国

中国民族摄影艺术出版社

美丽的 中國

目录 Contents

The Charms of China

美丽的中國

目录 Contents

The Charms of China

前　言

中国，疆域辽阔，自然地理环境复杂而丰富多彩。在辽阔的土地上，不仅有雄伟广袤的高原、纵横绵亘的高山、茫茫无垠的沙漠，更有巨大富饶的盆地，一目千里的平原、美丽广阔的草原，以及奔腾不息的大川、烟波浩渺的湖泊，真是山河壮丽，气象万千。虽然构成中国众多奇景的基本要素仅仅为山和水，但是就像三原色组成了五彩缤纷的世界一样，大自然通过山和水的不同组合、不同姿态，在中国大地上造就了无数极具审美情趣的胜景，将山魂水魄展现得淋漓尽致，将山情水韵升腾到完美境界。

地形概况

中国地势西高东低，呈阶梯状分布。滔滔黄河、滚滚长江，均发源于西部青藏高原群山之中，一路向东奔流，分别注入渤海和东海，即可反映出这一点。中国地形多种多样，高原、山地、丘陵、盆地、平原这五种地形都有大面积分布，各自呈现出不同的自然景观，就海拔高度而言，大致可分为四级阶梯。

青藏高原，平均海拔4000米以上，被誉为"世界屋脊"，是中国地形上最高一级的阶梯。高原上分布着许多高山、冰川，主要有昆仑山脉、阿尔金山脉、冈底斯山脉、祁连山脉、唐古拉山脉、喜马拉雅山脉等。在高原的山岭间镶嵌有许多水草丰美的草原，波光激滟的湖泊和大小不一的盆地。从青藏高原北缘的昆仑山—祁连山和东缘的岷山—邛崃山—横断山脉一线向东，地势迅速下降到海拔1000~2000米左右，形成了第二级阶梯，主要由内蒙古高原、黄土高原、云贵高原和塔里木盆地，准噶尔盆地、柴达木盆地、四川盆地构成。第三阶梯平均海拔500米~1000米以下，从大兴安岭、太行山、巫山和雪峰山向东直达海岸。这里自北向南分布着东北平原、华北平原和长江中下游平原。长江以南还有一片广阔的低山丘陵，一般统称为东南丘陵。再向东为中国大陆架浅海区，碧波一望无际，岛屿星罗棋布，这里水深大都不足200米，也被称作中国的第四级阶梯。

山地、丘陵

中国是一个多山的国家，山地，丘陵面积约占全国土地总面积的43%，不仅山区面积广大，而且大小山脉遍布全国，构成了中国地形的骨架，江河的流向和气候的差异都不同程度地受其影响。按走向大致可分为：东西走向、东北—西南走向、西北—东南走向和南北走向等几类。

东西走向的山脉是中国山脉中最主要的一类，主要有三列：从北至南分别为天山—阴山、昆仑山—秦岭、南岭。其中，南岭由五座山岭组成，横贯于广西、湖南、广东和江西四省边境，是长江水系和珠江水系的分水岭，也是东南丘陵的主干。

东北—西南走向的山脉，多在中国东部，也可分为三列，包括大兴安岭—太行山—雪峰山（即第二和第三阶梯的分界线）、长白山—武夷山和崛起于海上的台湾山脉。

西北—东南走向的山脉多分布于西部，主要有阿尔泰山、祁连山和喜马拉雅山。其中，喜马拉雅山脉位于青藏高原西南边缘，山势高峻雄伟，平均海拔高度达6000米以上，7000米以上的高峰就有40座之多。珠穆朗玛峰，海拔8844.43米，是世界最高峰，曾被人们与北极和南极相提并论，称为"地球第三极"。

中国南北走向的山脉不多，主要有横断山脉、贺兰山和六盘山等，其中尤以横断山脉表现最为显著。

中国丘陵多在东部地区广泛分布，主要有辽东丘陵、山东丘陵和东南丘陵，海拔在200~500之间。只有少数超过1000米，如山东省泰山，安徽省黄山和江西省庐山等。

冰川

中国是世界上山岳冰川最发达的国家之一。冰川分布地域广泛，北起阿尔泰山，南至云南丽江玉龙雪山，西自帕米尔高原，东到四川贡嘎山，跨越新疆、西藏、甘肃、青海、四川和云南等

六个省区，纵横2500千米，总面积约56500平方千米，占亚洲冰川总面积的40%，储水量达50000亿立方米。冰川既是天然的固体水库，又是极具吸引力的旅游资源。大自然鬼斧神工般地塑造了弧拱、塔林、桥梁、蘑菇、冰湖、冰瀑等千奇百怪的景观，奇巧多姿，形象生动。

高原、平原、盆地

中国的高原主要分布在大兴安岭—太行山—雪峰山一线以西地区，面积约占全国总面积的26%。青藏、云贵、内蒙古和黄土高原，是最著名的四大高原。青藏高原是世界上最高的高原，平均海拔4500米，面积近240万平方千米，包括西藏、青海、四川西部和新疆南部等广大地区，被誉为"世界屋脊"。内蒙古高原开阔坦荡，是中国第二大高原，面积约100万平方千米。高原西部气候干燥，降水较少，大部分为沙漠和戈壁；东部则牧草肥美，是中国最大的天然牧场。云贵高原平均海拔1000~2000米，主要在云南和贵州境内，广西、四川、湖北、湖南等省也有分布。云贵高原是长江、西江（珠江的最大支流）和元江三大水系的分水岭，高原上河流众多，因此形成了许多高深的峡谷。黄土高原横跨山西、陕西等六个省，总面积58万平方千米，是世界上黄土分布最广阔、最深厚，也是最典型的黄土地貌区，黄土层厚度达100米左右，最厚的地方可达200米。

长江、黄河、珠江和黑龙江等大河流，在辽阔的大地上奔流，造就了许多广大而肥沃的平原。中国的平原分布很广，总面积112万平方千米，约占全国土地面积的12%，主要分布在第三阶梯，著名的有东北大平原、华北大平原、长江中下游平原，以及珠江三角洲平原和台湾西部平原。他们主要是由江、河、湖、海的泥沙堆积而成，地势平坦，水网密布，土地肥沃，是中国重要的农耕地区。其中，东北大平原由三江平原、辽河平原和松嫩平原组成，总面积35万平方千米，是中国最大的平原。

中国由于山区面积广大，山脉纵横交错，在网格状的山脉间形成了许多的盆地。面积超过10万平方千米的盆地有塔里木盆地，准噶尔盆地、柴达木盆地和四川盆地。它们是中国著名的四大盆地，都分布在西部地区。

河流、湖泊

中国境内的河流，仅流域面积在1000平方千米以上的就有1500多条。中国河流的总长度达22万千米。主要河流多发源于青藏高原，落差很大，因此，中国的水利资源非常丰富。大部分河流自西向东，注入太平洋，主要河流有长江、黄河、黑龙江、海河、淮河、珠江等。其中，长江，全长6300千米，是中国第一大河，为世界第三大河；黄河，是中国第二长河，全长5464千米，被誉为"中华民族的摇篮"。流入印度洋的有怒江和雅鲁藏布江等。新疆境内的额尔齐斯河是我国惟一流入北冰洋的河流。

中国是个多湖的国家，有自然湖泊近2.5万个，其中面积在1平方千米以上的多达2800个，面积在1000平方千米以上的湖泊有13个。从东部沿海到西部高原，无论是湿润区还是干旱区，都有天然湖泊分布，但分布很不均匀，主要集中在东部平原、青藏高原、蒙新地区、东北平原与山地和云贵高原。尤其是东部平原和青藏高原的湖泊最多，约占全国湖泊总面积的81%以上。青海湖是咸水湖，面积4236.6平方千米，为中国最大的湖泊。中国著名的五大淡水湖分别是鄱阳湖、洞庭湖、太湖、洪泽湖和巢湖，其中鄱阳湖是中国最大的淡水湖。中国海拔最高的湖是西藏的纳木错，海拔最低的湖是新疆的艾丁湖，最长的湖泊是西藏的班公错，最深的湖是吉林长白山天池。

喀斯特地貌

在中国，从世界屋脊的青藏高原到海浪滔滔的台湾岛域，从林海雪原的大兴安岭到美丽富饶的南海诸岛，不论是巍巍群山，还是

宽广平原，都分布有许多绮丽的喀斯特地形。地面上有溶沟、峰林、溶石、天生桥、漏斗、竖井、洼地、溶盆，还有瀑布、悬挂泉、喀斯特湖、喀斯特潭等；地下世界则更加奇妙，有溶洞、地下河、暗湖及造型各异的钙质沉积形态，如石钟乳、石笋、石柱、石花、石幔、石瀑布、莲花盆等等。各种喀斯特地形，千姿百态，组成了绮丽多姿的广西桂林山水、柱石林立的云南石林、构造奇特的贵州贵阳地下公园、神奇梦幻的四川九寨沟风光、汩汩喷薄的山东济南趵突泉、层层叠叠的江苏宜兴善卷洞……把万里江山装扮得分外妖娆。贵州省是中国最大的一片喀斯特分布区，而广西桂林山水则应是最著名的景区了。

沙漠、戈壁

中国的沙漠、戈壁和沙漠化土地面积总计约130多万平方千米，占国土面积的13.5%，主要分布在西北、华北北部及东北西部的七个省区，其中，以新疆分布的面积最广。中国著名的大沙漠主要有塔克拉玛干沙漠、古尔班通古特沙漠、库布齐沙漠、巴丹吉林沙漠、腾格里沙漠等。塔克拉玛干沙漠面积达33万平方千米，是中国最大的沙漠，也是世界上著名的大沙漠之一。

海岸、岛屿

中国不仅陆地面积辽阔，而且也是一个海洋浩瀚、岛屿众多、海岸线漫长的国家。中国大陆的东部与南部濒临渤海、黄海、东海和南海，海域面积473万平方千米，大陆海岸线长达18000多千米。在辽阔的海域上，分布着5000多座大小岛屿。其中，最大的是台湾岛，面积约3.6万平方千米；其次是海南岛，面积约3.4平方千米。

气候

中国领土跨越的纬度近50度，大部分地区处于温带，南方部分地区处于热带和亚热带，北部则靠近寒带。中国气候具有大陆性季风气候显著和气候复杂多样两大特征。冬季盛行偏北风，夏季盛行偏南风，四季分明，雨热同季。冬季，干寒的冬季风从西伯利亚和蒙古高原吹来，由北向南势力逐渐减弱，寒冷而干燥；夏季暖湿气流从海洋上袭来，形成高温多雨的状况。于是，众多的山水美景在春夏秋冬、日月晨昏、阴晴雨雪、晓雾夕霞的变化中，展现出风格迥异的别样魅力。

动物与植物

中国众多的灵山秀水，孕育了生态系统的各种生态类型，包括森林、草原、灌丛、草甸等，使中国成为物种资源最丰富的国家之一。仅高等植物就有3.2万种。北半球寒、温、热各带植被的主要植物，在中国几乎都可以看到。木本植物有7000多种，水杉、水松、银杉、杉木、金钱松、台湾杉、福建柏、珙桐（中国鸽子树）、杜仲、喜树等为中国所特有。中国还有食用植物2000余种、药用植物3000多种，以及众多花卉植物。中国也是世界上野生动物种类最多的国家之一，约有动物10万余种，占世界总数的10%以上。大熊猫、金丝猴、华南虎、褐马鸡、丹顶鹤、白鳍豚、扬子鳄等百余种中国特产的珍稀野生动物，闻名于世。

中国幅员辽阔，风景名胜皓若繁星，不胜枚举。我们从上千幅摄影作品中，精心挑选出200余幅最具代表性的图片，编辑成这本画册，向您展示壮美秀丽的中国风光。画册按大致地域分为东、南、西、北四个篇章，遴选不同季节，不同天气、不同角度的精美图片，并撰写了较为翔实的文字介绍，带您领略中国风光的无穷魅力。但若想将地大物博的中国胜景收录于一本画册，恐怕是"难于上青天"的，这是我们的遗憾。一位英国著名摄影大师是这样诠释他的摄影理念的："给观众展现得越少，能表现得东西就越多……可以让他们有更多遐想的空间。"引用于此，来表达我们的愿望。

Foreword

Situated in the eastern part of the Asian Continent, the People's Republic of China is one of the largest countries in the world with abundant resources and products, and complicated yet colorful physical geographic environment. These bestow China with enchanting natural landscape, including magnificent and extending plateaus, imposing and rolling mountains, boundless and attractive deserts, large and fruitful basins, limitless and flat plains, beautiful and endless grasslands, as well as rushing rivers and mist-covered lakes. Although, in a sense, the captivating scenery is simply formed by mountains and waters, the nature creates so many wonderful landscapes possessing great aesthetic values on vast land of China by means of different combination and various shapes, just as the three-primary colors create a multihued world. The souls of mountains and rivers are displayed thoroughly, and their emotions reach to the acme of perfection.

General Topography

The physical relief of China drops off in a series of escarpments eastward to the ocean. The surging Yellow River and rolling Yangtze River, both rising in mountains on the Qinghai-Tibet Plateau in the west of China but emptying into the Bohai and Donghai seas respectively in the east, reflect the feature. China's topography is varied and complicated, and plateaus, mountains, hills, basins and plains are widely distributed throughout the country, presenting different natural landscapes. Taking a bird's-eye view of China, the terrain gradually descends like a four-step staircase.

The top of the "staircase" is the Qinghai-Tibet Plateau, which is reputed as the "Roof of the World" with an average height of more than 4,000 meters above sea level. Standing on the plateau are many lofty mountains and glaciers including Kunlun, Altun, Gangdise, Qilian, Tanggula and Himalayas, scattering among which are prairies with lush grass, wavy lakes and basins of various sizes. From Kunlun and Qilian mountains at the northern edge of Qinghai-Tibet Plateau and Minshan, Qionglai and Hengduan mountain ranges at its eastern edge eastward is the second step with an average elevation of between 1,000 and 2,000 meters. It comprises primarily Inner Mongolia, Loess and Yunnan-Guizhou plateaus, and the Tarim, Junggar and Sichuan basins. The third step, about 500-1,000 meters in elevation, begins at a line drawn around the Daxing'anling (Greater Hinggan), Taihang, Wushan and Xuefeng mountain ranges and extends eastward to the coast. In the area, from north to south, are the Northeast Plain, the North China Plain and the Plain of the Middle and Lower Reaches of the Yangtze. Additionally, south to the Yangtze River are hills and foothills, and they are generally known as Foothills of Southeastern China. To the east, the land extends out into the ocean, in a continental shelf, the fourth step of the staircase. The water here is less than 200 meters deep. Many islands and isles are scattered in the vast expanse of seas.

Mountains and Hills

China is occasionally called the land of mountains. About 43 per cent of its territory is mountainous or hilly. Mountains and hills can be found all over the country, forming the skeleton of China's landform, which also affect local rivers' flow direction and different climate in varying degrees. According to the trend, they are roughly classified into four groups: east-west, northeast-southwest, northwest-southeast and south-north.

The east-west trending mountains are major ones in China, which are arranged in three rows. Going from north to south they are Tianshan and Yinshan mountains, Kunlun and Qinling mountains, as well as Nanling (Southern Mountain Ranges). Among them, the Nanling on the Guangxi-Hunan-Guangdong-Jiangxi border comprises 5 mountain ridges, and is trunk of hills in the southeast of China. Though not high, the Nanling range is a natural dividing line in southern China, separating the Yangtze River from the Zhujiang River.

Most of the northeast-southwest trending mountains are grouped in the low-lying east of China also in three rows: Daxing'anling, Taihang and Xuefeng mountains in the west, Changbai and Wuyi mountains in the middle, and the Taiwan Mountains rising on the sea in the east.

The northwest-southeast ranges, mostly in the west, include Altay, Qilian and Himalayas. The Himalayas lying principally in China on the southwestern edge of Qinghai-Tibet Plateau is the most majestic and highest mountain range in the world. The main chain of Himalayas has an average elevation of more than 6,000 meters, far exceeding the average height of any other mountain range in the world. As many as 40 Himalayan peaks are more than 7,000 meters above sea level, among which, the Mount Qomolangma towering 8,844.43 meters is the highest in the world and is reputed "the Third Pole" of the earth.

There are not much south-north ranges in China, and the Helan and Liupan mountains in Ningxia and other provinces and the Hengduan Mountains straddling Sichuan, Yunnan and Tibet are most famous. The Himalayas join with the Hengduan and other ranges to form a huge arc-shaped mountain chain.

Hills are widely distributed in the east of China, such as Liaodong Hills, Shandong Hills and Southeast Hills. All of them are 200 meters to 500 meters in elevation, except few are over 1,000 meters high including Taishan in Shandong, Huangshan in Anhui and Lushan in Jiangxi.

Glaciers

China is one of counties boasting most developed glaciers in the world. From the Altay Mountains in the north to the Yulong Snow Mountain in Yunnan Province in the south, and from the Gongga Mountain in Sichuan Province in the east to the Pamirs Plateau in the west, glaciers are widely dispersed in six provinces or autonomous regions in China including Xinjiang, Tibet, Gansu, Qinghai, Sichuan and Yunnan. Covering an area of 56,500 square kilometers, or 40 per cent of Asia's total glaciers area, the glaciers in China has ice storage of approximately 5 trillion cubic meters. Abundant glaciers are not only natural solid reservoirs, but also attractive tourist resource. In many a legend and many a shape, they magically resemble arches, pagoda forests, bridges, mushrooms, icy lakes, and icy waterfalls and so on, very vividly.

Plateaus, Plains and Basins

Plateaus cover about 26 per cent of China's total area, mainly in its western and central parts, or the first and second steps of the topographical staircase. The four great ones are the Qinghai-Tibet, Yunnan-Guizhou, Inner Mongolia and Loess plateaus. Having an average elevation of 4,500 meters, the Qinghai-Tibet Plateau in western and southwestern China is the highest plateau in the world, embracing the whole of Tibet, Qinghai, western Sichuan and south Xinjiang— an area of nearly 2.4 million square kilometers. It is reputed as the "Roof of the World". The Inner Mongolia Plateau is the second largest plateau in China with a total of more than one million square kilometers. Western part of the plateau, principally consisting of deserts and gobi, is characterized by dry climate with less precipitation; while the eastern part is covered with lush grass, making it an ideal natural grazing land. The Yunnan-Guizhou Plateau covering eastern Yunnan, the greater part of Guizhou as well as such provinces of Guangxi, Sichuan, Hubei and Hunan, is at an elevation of 1,000-2,000 meters. It forms the watershed of three river systems: the Yangtze, Xijiang (largest tributary of Zhujiang River) and Yuanjing. The crisscross rivers cut mountain areas into numerous high and steep canyons sandwiched between towering peaks, making the plateau surface rugged and uneven. The Loess Plateau, spanning 6 provinces including Shanxi and Shaanxi covers an area of 580,000 square kilometers. It is the largest loess plateau in the world with deepest layer of loess, which is generally 100 meters deep and some places exceed 200 meters.

The Yangtze River, Yellow River, Zhujiang, Heilongjiang and other great river gallop on the vast expanse of land of China, bringing up many extensive and fertile plains. Widely distributed, they cover 1.12 million square kilometers, or about 12 per cent of the country's total area. Most famous plains lie in the northeast and eastern seaboard regions, including the Northeast, the North China, and the Middle-Lower Yangtze River, Zhujiang Delta and Western Taiwan plains. Created by mud and silt from the rivers and their tributaries, lakes or seas, these plains, with a gentle terrain, fertile soil, mild climate, as well as densely network of rivers and streams, provide a base for China's major agriculture and farming. Among them, the Northeast Plain, consisting of Sanjiang, Liaohe and Songnen plains, covers a total of 350,000 square kilometers and is the largest of China's plains.

Scattering among the extensive mountainous area and interlocking mountains are many basins. The largest ones – Tarim, Dzungar, Chaidamu (Tsaidam or Qaidam) and Sichuan – are all lying in the west of China and larger than 100,000 square kilometers.

Rivers and Lakes

China abounds in rivers, which totally lengthening about 220,000 kilometers. More than 1,500 rivers each drain 1,000 square kilometers or larger areas. A few large rivers rise from the Qinghai-Tibet Plateau with big drops, making China leading the world in hydroelectric power potential. Because China's terrain is high in the west and low in the east, most of its rivers flow east and empty into the Pacific Ocean, including the Yangtze, Yellow, Heilongjiang, Haihe, Huaihe, Zhujiang rivers. Among them, the Yangtze, 6,300 kilometers in length, is the largest river in China, and the third longest in the world; the 5,464-kilometer-long Yellow River, the second longest river in China, is reputed as one of the "Cradle of the Chinese Civilization". The Nujiang and Yarlung Zangbo rivers in the south of the Qinghai-Tibet Plateau flow south out of China into the Indian Ocean, and the Ertix River in the northwest corner of Xinjiang flows into the Arctic Ocean.

China is a land of many lakes. A total of nearly 25,000 natural lakes are found both in the warm, humid plains of the east and the clod, high regions of the west. Over 2,800 lakes exceed one square kilometer, of which more than 13 exceed 1,000 square kilometers. Yet, the distribution of lakes in China is non-uniform. Most of lakes are concentrated in the plains in the east of the country, Qinghai-Tibet Plateau, and the rest are scattered in the Yunnan-Guizhou Plateau, the Inner Mongolia Plateau, Xinjiang and the northeast. Total area of lakes in the eastern plains and on the Qinghai-Tibet Plateau accounts for over 81 per cent of the whole lake area of China. The Qinghai Lake (salt water lake) having an area of 4236.6 square kilometers is the largest lake in China; while Poyang Lake ranks first among the five largest freshwater lake of China, the other four being Dongting, Taihu, Hongze and Chaohu. The highest lake in China is Namco Lake in Tibet, the lowest Aiding Lake in Xinjiang, the longest lake Banggong in Tibet, while the deepest is the Heavenly Lake on summit of Changbai Mountain in Jiling Province.

Karst

From the Qinghai-Tibet Plateau, Roof of the World, eastward to the Taiwan Island surrounded by surging sea, and from the snow-land of Daxing'anling southward to the beautiful and fertile islands in the South Sea, Karst topography is widely distributed in China. They exist in various forms and shapes, such as gullies, peak forests, rocks, bridges, funnels, potholes, depressions, basins, as well as waterfalls, hanging springs, lakes and pools on the earth surface. Yet, the world underground is much wonderful. There were karst caves, subterranean streams, underground lakes, and what's more calcareous deposits and stalactites resembling bamboo shoots, pillars and columns, flowers, curtains, waterfalls, basins and so on. They bring up the beautiful scenery of Guilin in Guangxi, the Stone Forest in Yunnan, magical Underground Park in Guizhou, dreamlike world of Jiuzhaigou in Sichuan, gushing Baotu Spring in Shandong, overlapping caves in Shanjuan Cave in Jiangsu, and others, each having a role to play in beautifying the country. In Guizhou, 73 per cent of topography is made of the Karst landform, which makes it the province possessing largest area of karst in China, and perhaps the scenery of Guilin is the most famous attraction of karst.

Deserts

The deserts, gobis and desertificated land in China, totaling more than 1.3 million square kilometers, make up 13.5 per cent of its total territory. They are distributed mainly over 7 provinces or autonomous regions in the northwest, north and northeast of China, and among them, Xinjiang possesses largest desert area. The well-known deserts in China include Taklamakan, Gurbantungut, Kubqi, Patanchilin, and Tengger deserts. The Taklamakan Desert with an area of 330,000 square kilometers is the largest in China and one of the most famous deserts in the world.

Seaboard and Islands

China boasts not only vast land area, but also seas stretching to the horizon, multitudinous islands and isles, as well as long coastline. The China's mainland is flanked to the east and south by the Bohai, Yellow, East China and South China seas, with a total maritime area of 4.73 million square kilometers and a coastline of 18,000 kilometers. Scatted on the vast Chinese territorial seas are more than 5,000 islands in varying sizes. The largest of these, with an area of about 36,000 square kilometers, is Taiwan, followed by Hainan with an area of 34,000 square kilometers.

Climate

The vast territory of China spans nearly 50 latitudinal degrees, and most of it is in the Temperate Zone, with a small part extending south into the Tropical and Subtropical zones and the northernmost tip close to the Frigid Zone. China has a marked continental monsoon climate characterized by great variety. Northerly winds prevail in winter, while southerly winds reign in summer. The four seasons are quite distinct. The rainy season coincides with the hot season. In winters, the dry and cold winter monsoons from Siberia and Mongolia in the north gradually become weak as they reach the southern part of the country, resulting in cold and dry winters and great differences in temperature; while in summers, the warm and moist summer monsoons from the oceans bring abundant rainfall and high temperatures. Therefore, unmatched scenery of China is bestowed with different charms that survive the charge of seasons throughout a year, of hours in a day, and of different weather.

Fauna and Flora

Thanks to the countless mountains and waters, China has a quite complete ecosystem, which includes various ecological types such as forest, grassland, bush-woods and grassy marshlands and enable the land to be one of the countries with the greatest diversity of species resource in the world. There are more than 32,000 species of higher plants, and almost all the major plants that grow in the northern hemi-sphere's frigid, temperate and tropical zones are represented in China. The country has 7,000 species of woody plants, of which 2,800 are arbors. The metasequoia, Chinese cypress, Cathay silver fir, China fir, golden larch, Taiwan fir, Fujian cypress, dove-tree, eucommia and camplotheca acuminata are found only in China. In addition, China is home to more than 2,000 species of edible plants, 3,000 species of medicinal plants, and a wide variety of flowering plants. China is also the country having most abundant wildlife resource in the world. There are more than 4,400 species of vertebrates, more than 10 per cent of the world's total. Wildlife peculiar to China includes such well-known animals as the giant panda, golden-haired monkey, South China tiger, brown-eared pheasant, white-flag dolphin, Chinese alligator and red-crowned crane, totaling more than 100 species.

Through abundant and elegant pictures, as well as detailed introduction, this photo-album showcases splendid and graceful sceneries in China in four parts: the East, the South, the West and the North, roughly according to their geographic locations. Yet, China boasts so many charming scenic spots that no one album could include all of them. We had to handpick 200-odd photographic works taken in different seasons and weathers and at different angles from more than 1,000 thousands pictures, at the same time we cannot but feel pity for it. However, an English master of photographing once expressed his photographing idea: "The less I show in my picture, the more it displays······ which enable views to have much more imagination." That is also our wish to compile this album.

云南省三江并流景区：梅里雪山
**Meili Snow Mountain of the Three
Parallel Rivers of Yunnan Protected Areas**

East China

美丽的中国·东部

安徽省 Anhui Province

山东省 Shandong Province

浙江省 Zhejiang Province

江苏省 Jiangsu Province

福建省 Fujian Province

上海市 Shanghai Municipality

东

国东部主要旅游景区简介：

九华山：位于安徽省青阳县西南20千米处，山势雄伟，群峰竞秀，与五台山、峨眉山、普陀山合称"中国佛教四大名山"。九华山风光诗旎，气候宜人，是消夏避暑的胜地。景区面积120平方千米，有大小山峰99座，其中以天台、天柱、十王、莲花等9座山峰最著名。十王峰为最高峰，海拔1342米。九华山水质清澈，泉、池、潭、瀑众多，散布在奇峰深谷、怪石古洞、苍松翠竹之间，绮丽清幽，相映成趣。九华山上古刹林立，香烟缭绕，是佛教的圣地，专为地藏王菩萨的道场。秀美的自然风光与浓郁的佛教气氛，使九华山享有"东南第一山"的美誉，每年，国内外慕名旅游、朝圣者不可胜数。

泰山：五岳之东岳，古称岱宗、岱山，位于山东省中部，以雄伟壮丽著称，自然风光极为优美。因历代帝王登基之初，多来泰山举行封禅大典、祭告天地，而享有"五岳独尊"之美誉。无论是帝王将相，还是名人宗师，都对泰山仰慕备至。孔子"登东山而小鲁，登泰山而小天下"传为佳话，杜甫"会当凌绝顶，一览众山小"，亦成千古绝唱。泰山风景区总面积125平方千米，分为幽、旷、秀、奥、妙等五大景区，最高峰玉皇顶海拔1545米。泰山山势挺拔，奇峰突兀，在苍松巨石、云岚雾影、幽潭飞瀑的衬托之下，雄浑之中兼有明丽，壮阔之中透着秀丽，成为我国山水名胜的集大成者。云海和日出是其两大自然奇观。1987年，泰山被联合国教科文组织列为世界自然与文化双重遗产。

普陀山：雄峙于浙江省杭州湾以东约100海里的莲花洋中的海岛之上，是中国佛教四大名山之一，也是著名的海岛风景旅游胜地。全岛面积约12.5平方千米，呈狭长形，最高处佛顶山，海拔约300米。普陀山上，海景变幻，洞幽岩奇，古刹琳宫，云雾缭绕，名胜古迹比比皆是，享有"以山而兼湖之胜，则推西湖；以山而兼海之胜，当推普陀"的评价。普陀山素有"海天佛国"之称，为观音菩萨的道场，最盛时拥有80余座庙宇。美丽的自然风景和浓郁的佛教气氛，使它蒙上一层神秘的色彩，吸引着众多的海内外游人香客。

楠溪江：为国家级风景名胜区，位于浙江省温州市永嘉县北，景观丰富，融天然山水、田园风光和人文景观于一体，以"水秀、岩奇、瀑多、村古"著称，被誉为"中国山水画的摇篮"。楠溪江主流长约140千米，流域面积2400余平方千米，逶迤曲折，注入瓯江，流归东海，有36湾、72滩之称。景区总面积625平方千米，共分为楠溪江及沿江农村文化、大若岩、石桅岩、水岩、北坑、陡门和四海山二大景区，共有800多个景点。江水蜿蜒纯净，缓急有度，两岸滩林如黛，野趣天成；峰笔立、崖如削、洞悬壁的奇异景观，与柔美的江水形成强烈对比，好一派诗旎风光！

绍兴东湖：位于浙江省绍兴市东3.5千米处，以山青、水秀、石奇闻名，与杭州西湖、嘉兴南湖并称"浙江省三大名湖"。这里原为一座高约60米的青石山，从汉代起，石

的景观，宛如一座巧夺天工的 水石大盆景 。清代，在塘外修建了一条长堤，堤内成湖，堤外为河，水深岩奇，湖洞相连，亭榭岛屿，点缀其间，成为古城绍兴景色最为独特的游览名胜。游览区内还有陶公洞、喇叭洞、仙桃洞和霞川桥等名胜。

雁荡山：位于浙江省乐清市境内，总面积450平方千米，因山顶有湖，芦苇茂密，结草为荡，南归秋雁多宿于此而得名。雁荡山分为灵峰、三折瀑、灵岩、大龙湫、雁湖、显圣门、仙桥、羊角洞等8个景区，共有500多个景点。其中，东南部风景荟萃，"二灵一龙"（灵峰、灵岩、大龙湫）被称为"雁荡三绝"。雁荡风景区内奇峰嵯峨，怪石嶙峋，泉清水碧，飞瀑若练，古洞幽深，茂林密布。大龙湫瀑布落差达190余米，气势磅礴，堪称奇观，是我国最著名的瀑布之一，自古以来，许多诗人、文士、画家、旅行家都留下赞美的诗文。

太湖：位于江苏省南部、长江三角洲南缘，面积约2400平方千米，是我国第三大淡水湖。太湖流域，河网纵横交织，湖泊密集，组成了庞大的灌溉系统和内河水运网，同时还是我国重要的淡水水产基地，有"鱼米之乡"的美誉。太湖湖面烟波缥缈，风光以雄浑清秀著称。湖中大、小岛屿散立，连同沿湖的山峰和半岛，号称72峰，四季景色不同，晨暮意境迥然，构成了一幅山外有山，湖中有湖，山重水复，水山交融的天然美景，充满诗情画意。而太湖之胜尤在鼋头渚。鼋头渚位于太湖之滨的充山西端，因有石形如鼋头伸入湖中，故称，是赏日出、观日落以及欣赏太湖风光的绝佳之处。

武夷山：位于福建省北部、与江西省交界处，是由红色砂砾岩组成的低山丘陵，以丹霞地貌为主，有"奇秀甲东南"之称。风景区内山清水秀，溪谷环绕，自然风光优美，文化遗存众多，有"三三、六六、九九"之胜。"三三"指的是澄澈清莹、蜿蜒萦回的九曲溪；"六六"指的是夹岸林立、巍巍葱郁的36座青峰；"九九"则指的是星罗棋布、千姿百态的99座山岩。山临水立，水绕山转，碧水丹山，珍木灵草，奇岩古穴，飞禽走兽构成了武夷山奇幻百出的山水胜境，自古以来，吸引了无数帝王将相、骚人墨客、释道高人和艺术家。1999年，武夷山被联合国教科文组织列为自然与文化双重遗产。主要景点有九曲溪、大王峰、天游峰、一线天、玉女峰、水帘洞和武夷宫等。

Major scenic areas in the East China are as follows:

Jiuhua Mountain: About 20 kilometers southwest of Qingyang County in Anhui Province, the Jiuhua Mountain is of nationwide fame for its lofty and steep peaks. With the beautiful scenery and favorable climate, the mountain is an ideal summer resort. It supposed to be consisted of 99 peaks, 9 of which including the Tiantai (Heavenly Terrace), Tianzhu (Heavenly Pillar), Shiwang (Ten Kings) and Lianhua (Lotus Flower) are the most famous. The Shiwang Peak is the highest one with an altitude of 1,342 meters above sea level. Covering a total of 120 square kilometers, the scenic area is full of ridges and peaks, exotic-shaped rocks, ancient caves and luxuriant pines and bamboos, and scattering amongst them are beautiful water attractions including springs, ponds, pools and waterfalls. As the Bodhimanda of Ksitigarbha Bodhisattva, it is regarded as one of the four most important Buddhist Mountains, the other three being Wutai Mountain in Shanxi, Emei Mountain is Sichuan and Putuo Mountain in Zhejiang, and many ancient temples have been well-preserved till now. The graceful scenery and strong flavor of Buddhism win the mountain a reputation of the "Number One Mountain in the Southeast China", and lure countless tourists and pilgrims every year.

Taishan Mountain: Located at the central part of Shandong Province, Taishan Mountain, the East Sacred Mountain, was called Daizong or Daishan in ancient times, and is famous for the magnificent scenery. As the royal object of cult, Taishan Mountain was the venue where past emperors of various dynasties used to worship Heaven and Earth, and was thought to be the most famed one of the Five Sacred Mountains in China. Not only the emperors, generals and ministers, but also the sages, celebrity and literati all looked it up with admiration and have left countless inscriptions and steles there. Mencius once said: "When Confucius ascended the Dongshan Mountain, he realized how small the State of Lu was; while when he ascended the Taishan Mountain, he saw how small the empire was." And Du Fu (712—770) also described in his poem: "When I reach the Taishan and had a view, all any other mountain just was a hill." Covering an area of 125 square kilometers, the Taishan Mountain scenic resort comprises of Secluded, Spacious, Graceful, Secret, and Wonderful regions. The Yuhuangding (Jade Emperor Summit) is the highest peak with an elevation of 1,545 meters. The most spectacular features of the mountain are enjoying cloud-sea and sun rising. The majestic and splendid Taishan Mountain embodies the beautiful sights of famous mountains and waters in China. The intense grandeur from its breathtaking scenery exudes amazing elegance, astonishing profundity and immens

安徽省黄山云海
Sea of Clouds, Huangshan Mountain
Anhui Province

vastness, as well as an air of mystery. In 1987, the Taishan Mountain became a natural-and-cultural heritage site of the UNESCO.

Putuo Mountain: Located on the Lotus Flowers Sea, about 100 sea miles east to the Hangzhou Bay, Putuo Mountain is one of the four most famous Mountains of Buddhism as well as an attraction famous for island scenery. The long and narrow island covers an area of 12.5 square kilometers and the Fodingshan, the peak of the isle, rises about 300 meters above sea level. The Putuo Mountain's fascinating beauty is formed by the charming sea, secluded caves, strange-shaped rocks, curled clouds, ancient temples and countless historical sites. The mountain is often compared to the West Lake of Hangzhou:"No place is better than the West Lake in terms of the combined beauty of mountains and lakes; by the same token, no place is better than Putuo Mountain in terms of the combined beauty of mountains and the sea." The Putuo is said to be the Bodhimanda for Avalokitesvara Bodhisattva, and enjoys a reputation of the "Buddhist Kingdom on the Sea". In its heydays, there were more than 80 temples on the mountain. Beautiful scenery and strong flavor of Buddhist culture add the mountain a sense of mysteriousness, and attract many visitors.

Nanxi River: One of the national scenic resorts, Nanxi River is located north in Yongjia County, Wenzhou City, Zhejiang Province. Characterized by beautiful water, exotic rocks, various waterfalls and ancient villages, the resort is an integral whole of natural landscape, rural scenery and man-made scenic spots. It is famed as the "cradle of Chinese landscape painting". The Nanxi River zigzags its way 140 kilometers creating a 2,400-square-kilometer fertile drainage area of picturesque countryside. The river claiming to have 36 turns and 72 shoals flows into Oujiang River, which empties into the East China Sea at last. The Nanxi Scenic Resorts covers an area of 625 square kilometers and comprises of 7 tourist areas including Nanxi River and the village cultures along it, Daruo Rock, Stone Mast Rock, Water Rock, North Pit, Doumen and Four-Sea Mountain. There are a total of more than 800 scenic spots. The winding and limpid river flows in lively rhythm: sometimes slow while sometimes swift. The gentle and grace water makes a poignant contrast with the imposing peaks, razor-sharp cliffs and caves hanging precariously at the edge of cliffs.

East Lake in Shaoxing: The lake is located in the east suburbs of Shaoxing in Zhejiang Province, 5.5 kilometers from the city. Featuring an elegant landscape of lakes and mountains and fantastic stones, the lake, together with the West Lake in Hangzhou and the South Lake in Jiaxing, is known as one of the Three Famous Lakes in Zhejiang Province. The East Lake used to be a hill about 60 meters in height. From the Han Dynasty (206BC—220AD), stone-men had been there to quarry stones. After thousand years of excavation, parts of the hill were hollowed, forming a unique scene of lake where water is clear and rocks are exotic in shape. It is reputed as a huge potted landscape. During the Qing Dynasty (1644—1911), a dyke was built over the water, which divided the lake into a river outside and a lake inside. The beauty of the area is played up with the addition of isles, bridges and pavilions built in different periods of time. The East Lake is, in short, a famed tourist attraction in the lower Yangtze valley. The scenic area also includes Cave of Revered Mr. Tao, Horn Cave, Celestial Peach Cave, Glow-River Bridge, and other attractions.

Yandang Mountain: Located in Leqing City in southeastern Zhejiang Province, Yandang Mountain covers an area of 450 square kilometers, comprising of such eight scenic zones as Lingfeng (Spirit Peak), Three-Fold Waterfall, Lingyan (Spirit Crag), Dalongqiu (Great Dragon Pool), Yanhu (Wild Goose Lake), Xianshengmen (Sage-Presenting Gate), Xianqiao (Celestial Bridge) and Yangjiaodong (Cave of Ram's Horn), and more than 500 scenic spots. The word Yandang means "reed marsh for wild geese" in Chinese, and in autumn wild geese do gather in the marshes around the lake at the top of the mountain, hence the name. Towering peaks grotesque rocks, limpid springs, green pools, graceful waterfalls, ancient caves and luxuriant forests together form the enchanting landscape of Yandang Mountain. Among the countless scenic spots, the Lingyan, Lingshi and Dalongqiu Waterfall are considered the "three wonders of Yandang". Perhaps no waterfall here is more tremendous and majestic than the 190-meter-high Dalongqiu Waterfall, and many poems and articles have been composed or wrote on it by numerous poets, scholars, painters and travelers since ancient times.

Taihu Lake Scenic Area: With an area of 2,400 square kilometer, the Taihu Lake located in the south of Jiangsu Province and at the southern edge of Yangtze River Delta is the third largest freshwater lake in China. The drainage area of Taihu is crisscrossed by rivers and studded with lakes, which form an enor-

mous irrigation system and water transport network and an important basement of fresh water aquatic product. The area is known as the "land of fish and rice". Featured vast expanse of waters, the Taihu Lake is famous for spectacle yet delicateness. Isles and islands of various shapes are scattered in the lake, and are generally known as 72 Peaks together with the peaks and peninsulas by lake, which show different charm in different season. The area is remarkable for its poetical landscape. Outside a mountain are mountains; while inside a lake are lakes. Mountains and waters are in perfect harmony. Of many scenic spots of Taihu Lake, the Yuantouzhu (Turtle Head Islet) is the place most worth visiting. Located west to Chongshan Hill, it resembles a huge turtle stretching its head into the water, hence the name. It is the best place for watching the sun rising and sun setting, and provides a general view of the Taihu Lake.

Wuyi Mountain: The Wuyi Mountain Scenic Area is located in Wuyishan City and stretches along Fujian's northernmost border with Jiangxi Province. Possessing a well-preserved ecological environment on a *danxia* landform, the mountain encompasses a scenic retreat and a nature reserve and is imbued with a wealth of natural beauty and cultural interest, which win it a reputation of being the most scenic wonder in Southeast China. The attractions of Wuyi Mountain could be summed up by a few words: Three-Three Six-Six and Nine-Nine, which refer the zigzag and limpid Jiuquxi (Nine-Bend Stream), the wooded and graceful 36 peaks along the banks and the 99 rocks differing in thousands of shapes respectively. Paradise or not, with its jade-green water, red peaks, luxuriant vegetation, bizarre-shaped rocks, and countless birds and animals, the mountain surely represents one classic and popular genre of Chinese landscape Since ancient times, Wuyi Mountain has attracted an endless flow of emperors, officials, scholars, Taoist masters, Buddhist monks and travelers, as well as generations of painters and artists. In 1999, the UNESCO included it on the World Heritage List as a natural and cultural site. Main scenic spots include the Jiuquxi, Dawangfeng (Great King Peak), Tianyoufeng (Sky-Touring Peak), Yixiantian (A Thread of Sky), Yunufeng (Jade Maid Peak), Shuiliandong (Water Screen Cave) and Wuyigong (Wuyi Palace).

浙江省杭州市西湖
West Lake in Hangzhou
Zhejiang Province

安徽省黄山
Huangshan Mountain,
Anhui Province

黄山风景名胜区
Huangshan Mountain Scenic Area

黄山，中国十大风景名胜区之一，位于安徽省黄山市北约50千米处，古称黟山。传说中华民族的始祖黄帝轩辕氏在此修炼成仙，因此，唐代时改为今名。黄山风景区面积约1200平方千米，汇集奇峰72座，其中，天都峰、莲花峰和光明顶为黄山主峰，海拔均在1800米以上，雄姿灵秀，气势磅礴。1990年，黄山被联合国教科文组织列为世界文化与自然双重遗产。

黄山素有"天下名景集黄山"的盛誉，泰山之雄伟，华山之险峻，衡山之烟云，庐山之飞瀑，雁荡之巧石，峨嵋之秀丽，黄山无不兼而有之。明代旅行家、地理学家徐霞客两游黄山，曾留下"五岳归来不看山，黄山归来不看岳"的赞誉。黄山风景区属花岗岩峰林景观，山体峰顶尖陡，峰脚直落谷底，形成峰高峭拔、雄峻瑰奇的中高山地形。2004年，被联合国列入《世界地质公园网络名录》。

黄山以奇松、怪石、云海、温泉"四绝"著称于世。遍布黄山的松树，盘结于危岩峭壁之上，雄壮挺拔，姿态各异，层层叠叠，错落有致，显示出顽强的生命力。著名的有迎客松、送客松、黑虎松、凤凰松、团结松等。黄山巧石林立，怪岩遍布，或像人，或似物，形象生动，栩栩如生，带给游人无尽的想像，不禁赞叹大自然的鬼斧神工。黄山温泉，又称"朱砂泉"、"汤泉"，水质清澈，温度适宜，可饮可浴，自古便享誉四方。黄山尤以云海为奇。漫天的雨雾和层积云所构成的云海，诡异变幻，令人莫测，时而如轻纱拂遮，时而又如巨浪滔天；时而冉冉上升，时而在山腰飘忽；时而翻腾疾驰，时而飘逸舒卷……奇峰、古松、怪石在云海中忽隐忽现，似在天宇间游弋，又似在汪洋中沉浮，置身其中，犹如进入梦幻境地，令人飘飘欲仙。

黄山还兼有"天然动物园和植物园"的美称。黄山共有野生植物1400多种，植被覆盖率达82%以上，参天古木随处可见，多姿美观，也为动物繁衍生息提供了理想之所。500余种鸟类、珍禽类、爬行类、两栖类、鱼类动物生活在这里，野生动物资源极为丰富。

黄山拥有自然景点400余处，四季景色各异，晨昏晴雨，瞬息万变。绝妙的山水景观以及日出、晚霞、云海、佛光和雾凇等自然奇观各得其趣，真可谓人间仙境。

The Huangshan Mountain, one of the top ten celebrated scenic spots in China, is located in the north of Huangshan City of Anhui Province and about 50 kilometers from the city. Legend has it that Huangdi (Yellow Emperor), whose descendants all Chinese are supposed to be, made pills of immortality on the mountain known as Yishan Mountain at the time, so in the Tang Dynasty, it got its current name Huangshan (Yellow Mountain). Covering a total of 1,200 square kilometers, the mountain is said to have 72 peaks with different charms. Three main peaks — Tiandu (Celestial), Lianhua (Lotus Flower) and Guangmingding (Bright Summit)—are 1,800 meters or more above sea level. In 1990, the Huangshan Mountain was designated as a world natural and cultural heritage site by the UNESCO.

The Huangshan Mountain's scenery is based on its peak, and is a gathering place of nationwide beauties of famous mountains. The imposingness of Taishan, the precipitousness of Huashan, the misty scenes of Hengshan, the waterfalls of Lushan, the spectacular rocks of Yandang and gracefulness of Emei have all found their replicas on the Huangshan. No wander Xu Xiake (1587—1641), a noted traveler and geographer of the Ming Dynasty who traveled all the famous mountains and rivers, once praised "Having seen the five sacred mountains in China, one does not want to see any other mountains, while having seen the all-inclusive Huangshan Mountain, one does not with to see any of the five sacred mountains." Huangshan is formed on a huge body of granite. Erosion and vertical fracture resulted in lofty peaks and deep valleys, and the peaks present scenery of boundless variety, while the valleys feature slenderness, quietness and delicacy. Visitors on the mountain could enjoy the magnificent and precipitous landscapes created by granite masses and other natural beauties, which mingle harmoniously. In 2004, it was included in the Global Network of National Geoparks also by the UNESCO.

Huangshan's charm is composed of four key elements: fantastic pines, grotesque rocks, mysterious sea of clouds, and marvelous hot springs. Tall and straight pines, growing out of the rock cracks or standing adhering to the cliffs, could be found everywhere on the mountain. Upturning or overhanging, stretching or twisting, standing or crawling, these gnarled trees are luxuriantly green and each of them is in different shapes and has its own charm. The most famous ones include Guest-Greeting, Guest-Goodbye, Black Tiger, Phoenix, and Unity pines. The jagged rocks of Huangshan come in a variety of shapes. The big ones make rock forests while the small ones are exquisite. Some resemble human figures, some look like animals, simply beyond one's imagination. Lifelike and vividly, they are all natural works of art. The crystal clear hot spring on the mountain has been famous since ancient times, and formerly called cinnabar spring and the water is good for drinking and bathing. The rich mineral spring is of a high-temperature carbonate type with therapeutic effects for many diseases. Besides these, there is marvelous sea of clouds, which creates the fascination that no word can describe with different shapes: now fine gauze, now heavy sea; now rising slowly, now drifting freely; now turning and sweeping past, and now massing and scattering. The spectacular rocky peaks, odd-shaped ancient pines and queer rocks, shrouded in clouds and mist, seem like flying in sky or swimming in ocean. What a fairyland on the earth!

The Huangshan Mountain is a natural zoo and botanical garden. More than 82 per cent of the area is covered with over 1,400 species of plants. Luxuriant ancient trees offered an ideal place for wild animals, making the mountain a home to more than 500 kinds of birds, reptiles, amphibians and fishes.

Possessing 400 natural scenic spots, the Huangshan Mountain boasts exquisite scenery varying with the various seasons and weathers. The extremely beautiful scenery and natural phenomena of sun-rising, sunset glow, sea of clouds, Halo over the summit and the rime form an unpredictable wonderland.

安徽省黄山西海余晖
Beautiful Sunset of West Sea Scenic Area,
Huangshan Mountain, Anhui Province

安徽省黄山仙人踩高跷
Scenic Spot of "Immortal Walking on Stilts",
Huangshan Mountain, Anhui Province

安徽省黄山雾凇
Rimed Trees on the Huangshan Mountain,
Anhui Province

安徽省黄山迎客松
Guest-Greeting Pine on the
Huangshan Mountain, Anhui Province

安徽省九华山风光
Scenery of Jiuhua Mountain,
Anhui Province

山东省荣成市天尽头风景区
Scenic Area of "Ends of the Earth" in
Rongcheng City, Shandong Province

山东省泰山十八盘
Eighteen Mountain Bends of the
Taishan Mountain, Shandong Province

山东省青岛市总督府
Governor Mansion in Qingdao City,
Shandong Province

浙江省绍兴市东湖风景区
**East Lake Scenic Area in Shaoxing City,
Zhejiang Province**

浙江省雁荡山秋色
Yandang Mountain in Autumn,
Zhejiang Province

浙江省楠溪江渔歌唱晚
Nanxi River Bathed in the Glow of the
Setting Sun, Zhejiang Province

浙江省楠溪江之晨
Morning of Nanxi River Scenic Resort,
Zhejiang Province

1. 浙江省普陀山千步沙
   Qianbusha (Thousand-Pace Sands) of Putuo
   Mountain, Zhejiang Province

2. 浙江省普陀山夕照
   Putuo Mountain at Sunset, Zhejiang Province

3.浙江省富春江畔春色
Spring Scenery along the riverside of Fuchun
River, Zhejiang Province

4.浙江省建德市灵栖洞
Lingqi Cave in Jiande City, Zhejiang Province

浙江省千岛湖风光
Scenery of Qiandaohu (Thousand-Island Lake), Zhejiang Province

浙江省天台山飞瀑
Waterfall of Tiantai (Heavenly Terrace)
Mountain, Zhejiang Province

33

杭州西湖
West Lake in Hangzhou

美丽的西湖是我国著名的旅游胜地,位于浙江省杭州市西,以其秀丽的湖光山色和众多的名胜古迹而闻名中外,被誉为"人间天堂"。从古至今,众多文人墨客在此发思古幽情,留下不尽的诗文辞赋和美丽传说。

杭州西湖,三面环山,中涵碧水,湖区面积5.6平方千米,周长约15千米。著名的苏堤和白堤横亘在湖面,将西湖分割为5个大小不等的水域。湖面碧水荡漾,烟波浩渺,湖岸绿阴环抱,山色葱茏。西湖的魅力在于景因时变,四季不同,移步换景,胜趣无穷:晴可见潋滟,雨可观空蒙;春天群芳争艳,岸柳依依,夏天碧莲接天,青黛含翠,秋天天高气爽,桂香沁人,冬天暗香浮动,飞莺啼雪。游览西湖犹如行在画中,无怪乎宋代大文豪苏轼曾赞誉道:"水光潋滟晴方好,山色空蒙雨亦奇。欲把西湖比西子,淡妆浓抹总相宜。"

西湖的美,不仅在湖,也在于山。环绕西湖,花木繁茂,山峦叠翠,峰、岩、洞、壑无一不奇,泉、池、溪、洞无处不美。西湖西南有龙井山、南高峰、烟霞岭、大慈山、灵石山、南屏山、凤凰山、吴山等,总称南山;北面有灵隐山、北高峰、仙姑山、栖霞岭、宝石山等总称北山。山的高度都不超过400米,像众星捧月一般,拱卫着西湖这颗明珠。此外,虎跑、龙井、玉泉等名泉和烟霞、水乐、石屋等奇洞点缀于群山之间,给西湖风景区平添不少风韵,宛若人间仙境。

自古以来,依托西湖美景,在西湖内岛及湖边兴建了许多亭台楼阁,形成了一种疏朗开放型的古典园林分布格局,园林和自然景色浑然一体,相得益彰,西湖堪称一座完美的自然山水园林。在以西湖为中心的风景区内,分布着40多处风景名胜,主要由一山(孤山)、两堤(苏堤、白堤)、三岛(阮公墩、湖心亭、小瀛洲)、五湖(外西湖、北里湖、西里湖、岳湖和南湖)、十景(曲院风荷、平湖秋月、断桥残雪、柳浪闻莺、雷峰夕照、南屏晚钟、花港观鱼、苏堤春晓、双峰插云、三潭印月)构成。

Lying in the west of Hangzhou City in Zhejiang Province, the West Lake scenic zone features beautiful and unpredictable natural scenery, numberless scenic spots and historical sites, which has been luring countless painters and poets seeking tranquility and inspiration. It is one of the most famous attractions in China and has been nicknamed the "paradise on the earth" with myriad folk tales.

Embraced by emerald hills covered with lush forests on three sides, the limpid West Lake lies on west edge of Hangzhou and has a total area of 5.6 square kilometers and a circumference of 15 kilometers. Sudi Dyke and Baidi Dyke spread in the lake and divided it into five water bodies. The beauty of the West Lake lies in a lingering charm that survives the charge of seasons throughout a year and of hours in a day. What's more, whatever the season, the panorama is pleasing to the eye and the nuances of light shade together with the moods of the weather present an ever-changing picture that justifiably has been described as intoxicating. In spring, the gaily flowers are in full blossom accompanied by weeping willows; in summer, water surface is dotted with lotus flowers; in autumn, sweet osmanthuses send forth delicate fragrance; and in winter, snow covered the lake presenting a breathtaking scenery. No wonder Su Shi (1037—1101), a famous poet of the Northern Song Dynasty (960—1127), once compared the lake to Xizi (Xishi), an unrivalled beauty of the Spring and Autumn Period, in his poem, which reads: "Both beautiful when wavelets shimmering on a sunny day, or mountains shrouded in mist in the weather of rainy; Like Xizi whether dressed up with white and rose, or in plain grace she goes."

The blue smudge of hills that surrounds the lake lies under a cover of luxuriant trees and flowers. Peaks, rocks, caves and ravines each hold forth the fascination of unique scenery that compares favorable with the wonderland thanks to the addition of so many springs, pools, streams and brooks. They are so colorful and picturesque! The hills to the southwest of the lake include Dragon-Well Hill, South High Peak, Misty Glow Ridge, Miraculous Stone Hill, South Screen Hill, Phoenix Hill, Wushan Hill, and so on, which are collectively known as the South Hills; while to the north are Inspired Seclusion Hill, North High Peak, Female Celestial Hill, Glow-Dwelling Hill and Gemstone Hill, which all generally called the North Hills. No more than 400 hundred meters high, these hills set off the pearl-like West Lake as stars set off the moon. Additionally, the beautiful natural setting is enhanced by famous springs such as the Tiger Running, the Dragon-Well and the Jade, as well as mystical caves including Misty Glow, Water Interest and Stone House.

The West Lake is actually a well-preserved natural garden. Since ancient times, large numbers of pavilions, terraces, kiosks and water-houses have been constructed on the isles and the lakeside. The result has been a string of classical gardens that are picturesquely scattered and integrated with the natural beauty of the lake. Centered by the West Lake, the tourist area is strewn with more than 40 major scenic sites, which are formed principally by one hill (Gushan or Isolated Hill), two dykes (Sudi and Baidi), three isles (Ruangongdun, or Mound of Revered Mr. Ruan, Huxinting or Mid-Lake Pavilion, and Xiaoyingzhou, or Lesser Fairy Island of Yingzhou), five lakes (West Outer Lake, North Inner Lake, West Inner Lake, Yuehu Lake and South Lake) and ten beautiful sights (Lotus in the Breeze at Crooked Courtyard, Autumn Moon on Calm Lake, Melting Snow at Broken Bridge, Listening to Orioles Singing in the Willows, Sunset Glow over Leifen Peak, Evening Bell at Nanping Hill, Viewing Fish at Flowers Harbor, Spring Dawn at Sudi Causeway, Twin Peaks Piercing the Clouds, and Three Pools Mirroring the Moon).

浙江省杭州市西湖之夏
**Summer Scenery of the West Lake in
Hangzhou City, Zhejiang Province**

36

浙江省杭州市西湖春色
West Lake in Spring, Hangzhou City, Zhejiang Province

上海市黄浦江畔
**Bank of Huangpu River in
Shanghai Municipality**

1.江苏省宜兴市张公洞
Zhanggong Cave in Yixing City,
Jiangsu Province

2.江苏省宜兴市善卷洞
Shanjuan Cave in Yixing City,
Jiangsu Province

3.江苏省太湖帆影
Sails on the Taihu Lake, Jiangsu
Province

福建省武夷山风景区：九曲溪
Jiuquxi (Nine-Bend Stream) of Wuyi Mountain
Scenic Resort, Fujian Province

俯瞰福建省武夷山风景区
Overlooking the Wuyi Mountain
Scenic Resort, Fujian Province

福建省武夷山风光
Scenery of Wuyi Mountain,
Fujian Province

South China

美丽的中国·南部

湖南省 Hunan Province

湖北省 Hubei Province

河南省 Henan Province

江西省 Jiangxi Province

广东省 Guangdong Province

海南省 Hainan Province

广西壮族自治区 Guangxi Zhuang Autonomous Region

台湾省 Taiwan Province

香港特别行政区 Hong Kong Special Administrative Region

澳门特别行政区 Macao Special Administrative Region

南

中国南部主要旅游景区简介：

衡山：坐落于湖南省中部衡阳市境内，是著名的五岳之一的"南岳"和道教五大名山之一。衡山山势雄伟，南至衡阳，北到长江，盘行400余千米，共有72峰。主峰祝融峰，海拔1290米，上接苍穹，下临深壑，登临其上，远山近黛，尽收眼底，尤为壮观，也是观赏日出、云海的最佳处。祝融峰之高，藏经殿之秀，方广寺之深，水帘洞之奇被誉为"衡山四绝"。衡山历史悠久，古刹、碑刻等文物古迹众多，主要景点有祝融殿、藏经殿、南岳大庙、方广寺、南台寺、鬼镜台等。衡山群峰峥嵘，古木参天，云海漂浮，亭台掩映，绿草如茵，芳香竞谷，历来被称为"五岳独秀"。

神农溪：神农架位于湖北、陕西、四川三省的边界，属大巴山脉，南濒长江，北望武当山。相传远古时代，神农氏曾在这里遍尝百草，为民除病，由于山高峰陡，不得不搭架攀山采药，因而得名。全区面积3250平方千米，海拔超过3000米的高峰有6座，是我国原始森林之一。这里有山川交错的绮丽景色，有优美动人的神话传说，仅植物种属就达2000多种，其中珍贵植物30多种；野生动物500多种，其中列入国家保护的珍贵动物20多种。而当地神秘的"野人"传闻更是引人入胜。1978年，在大小神农架诸峰周围20平方千米的地带建立自然保护区，主要保护金丝猴、珙桐等珍稀动植物和森林生态系统。神农溪发源于神农架南坡，为长江支流。它全长60千米，沿途接纳20余处溪洞和瀑布，向南穿行于深山溪谷之中，注入浩浩长江。美流清洌明净，曲折迂回，两岸奇峰对峙，松柏滴翠，山花溢芳，群猴嬉戏，野趣横生。乘舟徜徉其间，宛若进入美丽的画廊，充满诗情画意，可以寻到一丝心灵的宁静。

武当山风景名胜区：武当山古名太和山，位于湖北省丹江口市，面临丹江口水库，背依神农架林区，绵延400多千米，山势雄伟。风景区面积约240平方千米，有72峰、36岩、24涧、9泉等胜景，灵岩奇洞幽藏其间，白云绿树交相辉映，蔚为奇观。主峰天柱峰海拔1612米，峻峭秀丽，其余各峰均倾向天柱，犹如拱拜朝圣。武当山不仅风光绮丽，也是中国道教名山和武当拳术的发源地，传说道教真武大帝在此得道飞升。山上有历代文物古迹和明代所建的道教建筑群，规模宏大，庄严绮丽。1994年，武当山古建筑群被联合国教科文组织列入《世界遗产名录》。主要景点有金殿、紫霄宫、元和观和南岩等。

西陵峡：西陵峡位于湖北省宜昌市，是长江三峡中最长、景色最美的一峡。其中，从宜昌南津关到秭归县香溪口的一段，长约76千米，以礁石林立、滩险水急、波涛汹涌而闻名，素称"鬼门关"。峡谷内，两岸怪石嶙峋，险崖峭立，有兵书宝剑峡、牛肝马肺峡、黄牛峡、灯影峡、青滩、泄滩、崆岭滩等名峡险滩，以及古代巴人岩棺遗迹、三游洞和陆游泉等古迹。在西陵峡沿岸山上，屹立有4块岩石，犹如赴西天取经的唐僧师徒四人：手搭凉蓬、前行探路的孙悟空；捧着肚皮、一步三晃的猪八戒；肩落重担、紧步相随的沙和尚；安然坐骑、合掌缓行的唐僧。形象逼真、惟妙惟肖，相视如生，妙不可言。

嵩山：为五岳之中岳，位于河南省登封市境内，是国家重点风景名胜区和国家地质公园。嵩山以险峻著称，东部称为太室山，西部称少室山。两山绵延近百千米，共有72座山峰，主峰峻极峰海拔近1500米。景区内层峦叠嶂，悬崖峭壁，林木葱郁，景象万千，异常壮美，自古即以"八景"、"十二胜"著名。而因其为少林武术的发源地，嵩山更是名扬四海。嵩山不仅是自然美景荟萃之地，也是人文景观的宝库，文化遗迹，比比皆是。其中，最为著名的景点有"天下第一名刹"——少林寺、中国现存最早的砖塔——嵩岳寺塔、中国最大的塔林——少林寺塔林、中国古代四大书院之一——嵩阳书院等等。

三清山：位于江西省东部玉山县北50千米处，主峰玉京峰海拔1817米。因玉京、玉华、玉虚三峰峻拔，犹如道教所尊玉清、上清、太清三尊，故以三清命名，是我国道教名山之一，被誉为"江南第一仙山"。风景区总面积220平方千米，有山峰48座，怪石近百处，景色绮丽，尤以奇峰怪石、苍松古树、云雾佛光、飞瀑流泉等自然风光最为引人入胜。山上景致的特点是：东险西奇、北秀南绝、中峰巍峨。群山姿态万千，摩天峥嵘，妙趣横生，其中，观音听曲、司春女神和巨蟒出山被誉为"三清山三绝"。

七星岩风景区：位于广东省肇庆市北约4千米处，面积约8平方千米，主要由星湖和七星岩组成，自古以来就有"峰险、石异、洞奇、庙古"之说。星湖碧涛荡漾、烟云缭绕、浩瀚似海：阆凤岩、玉屏岩、石室岩、天柱岩、蟾蜍岩、仙掌岩、阿坡岩七座具有浓郁南国风韵的山岩散布其间，座座峻秀可爱，林木苍翠，形态不同，排列如北斗七星，景区因此得名。七星岩风景区内长堤蜿蜒，古洞神奇，湖光山色，绰约多姿，风景独好，享有"桂林之山、西湖之水"的美誉。主要旅游景观有七岩、八洞、五湖、六岗，景点多达80个。

鼎湖山风景区：鼎湖山位于广东省肇庆市东北18千米处，是岭南四大名山之首，因山顶有湖，四时不涸，故名顶（鼎）湖。也有民间传说因黄帝曾在山顶铸鼎而得名。整个景区由鼎湖、三宝、凤来、鸡笼等十多座山峰组成，主峰鸡笼山海拔约1000米，是珠江三角洲地区的最高峰。从山麓到山顶依次分布着沟谷雨林、常绿阔叶林、亚热带季风常绿阔叶林等森林类型，因其特殊的研究价值闻名海内外，被誉为华南生物种类的"基因储存库"和"活的自然博物馆"。又因地球上北回归线穿过的地方大都是沙漠或干草原，中外学者将鼎湖山称作"北回归线上的绿宝石"，并被联合国教科文组织列入"人与生物圈计划"保护区。

西樵山风景名胜区：位于广东省佛山市南海区的西南部，距广州68千米，是珠江三角洲的一颗明珠。风景区面积约14平方千米，断崖峭壁，回溪叠壑，共有72峰、36洞和28瀑之胜，峰峰苍翠，洞洞藏幽，瀑鸣如歌，更有湖、泉、洞、岩、潭、台点缀其间，兼之林深苔厚，郁郁葱葱，奇景深藏，清幽秀丽，为它赢得了"南粤名山数二樵"的盛誉。清朝时，"西樵云瀑"即被列入"羊城八景"，西樵山……

如画的风景，美妙的大樱和动人的传说，吸引了无数文人墨客寻古探幽、吟诗作赋、挥毫刻碑，在此留下了大量赞美的名诗佳句。

东郊椰林：海南省位于中国最南端，北隔琼州海峡与广东省相望，为中国第二大岛，风光秀丽，气候宜人，是中国著名的热带风光旅游胜地。辽阔广袤的大海，绮旎秀丽的热带风光，明媚的阳光，碧蓝的天空，金色的沙滩，葱茏的椰林和柔软的海风，使游客产生梦幻般的遐想，在大自然中留连忘返。位于文昌市东郊镇的东郊椰林就是椰风海韵的典型景区。东郊椰林素有"椰林长城"之称，是中国十大海滨风光之一。当地有句俗话："文昌椰子半海南，东郊椰林最风光"，可见其名。在这里生长着红椰、青椰、高椰、水椰等品种的50余万株椰树，海风吹来，绵亘十余里的椰树林带如同波涛，此起彼伏，又似少女婆娑起舞，妩媚多姿，极具魅力。

南湾猴岛：位于海南省陵水黎族自治县境内。猴岛横卧海湾之中，气候温和，风光秀丽。全岛面积约10平方千米，三面临海，形状狭长。岛上树木成阴，灌木丛生，岩洞遍布，椰子、荔枝、菠萝蜜、杨桃等果树比比皆是，草木四季常青，是猕猴理想的生存之所。1965年，建立猕猴自然保护区，千余只猕猴在此生息繁衍，跳跃玩耍、争斗厮闹，常惹得游人捧腹大笑。岛上生态资源丰富，生物多样性强，有热带植物近400种，除珍贵动物猕猴外，还有水鹿、水獭、穿山甲等近20种兽类和鸥鹉、戴胜等30种鸟类，以及蟒蛇、蜥蜴等爬行类动物。

德天瀑布：德天瀑布位于广西壮族自治区崇左市大新县境内，横跨中、越两国，紧邻越南板约瀑布，是亚洲第一、世界第二大跨国瀑布。瀑布源起广西靖西县归春河，流入越南又流回广西。瀑布上游，河水迂回曲折，时分时合，水流至此突遇断崖，飞泻而下，一波三折，磅礴激荡，犹如一条巨大的银练，悬挂于峡谷之上，蔚为壮观。水量充足时，瀑布宽达200米，落差70余米，轰鸣震魄，声传数里。瀑布景观随四季变化，风姿各异。如遇晴日，水雾弥漫蒸腾，彩虹横跨，光彩夺目，使人如入仙境。

Major scenic areas in the South China are as follows:

Hengshan Mountain: Hengshan, named the Southern Mountain of the Five Sacred Mountains, is located in Hengyang County, the middle part of Hunan Province. It is one of the Five Most Famous Mountains of Taoism. Its 72 peaks form a range serpentining for as far as 400 kilometers from Hengyang in the south to the Yangtze River in the north. The main peak, Zhurong...

湖南省张家界天子山
Tianzi (Heavenly Son) Mountain of Zhangjiajie, Hunan Province

peak, rises 1,290 meters high, whose top commands a panoramic view of the mountain range and is a wonderful vantage point for viewing the sunrise and sea of clouds. The Southern Sacred Mountain enjoys a long history and was visited by many emperors and celebrities, which has bestowed it abundance of cultural relics such as halls, monasteries and stone inscriptions. Main tourist spots include Zhurong Hall, Hall of Storing Sutras, Nanyuedamiao (Temple of Southern Sacred Mountain), Fangguangsi (Square and Broad Temple), Nantaisi (Temple of South Terrace), Mojingtai (Magic Minor Terrace), and so on. The tallness of Zhurong Peak, the gracefulness of Hall of Storing Sutras, the seclusion of Fangguangsi and the wonder of Water Curtain Cave are reputed as four marvelous spectacles of the mountain. With steep and soaring peaks, towering ancient trees, shrouding clouds and mist and splendid architectures in harmony with green grass and fragrant flowers, Hengshan leads the five sacred mountains by its gracefulness.

Shennong Stream: Located at the juncture of Hubei, Shaanxi and Sichuan provinces, the Shennongjia faces the Yangtze River to the south and Wudang Mountain to the north. It belongs to the east branch of the Dabashan Mountains. Legend has it that when Shennongshi, a legendary emperor in ancient times, came here to gather medicinal herbs, he found the mountains were so high and steep that he had to climb it with the help of a frame, hence the name Shennongjia, which means Shennong's Frame in Chinese. Covering an area of 3,250 square kilometers, the area boasts 6 peaks 3,000 meters above sea level. It is one of virgin forests in China featuring beautiful landscape of mountains and rivers, moving stories and folktales. In the area grows more than 2,000 species of plants, of which more than 30 are rare ones. It is also home to more than 500 kinds of animals, and 20 of them are under state protection. The local rumor about wild man adds a mysterious appeal and makes the area a coveted venue for explorers. In 1978, a 20-square-kilometer reserve was established around the Big and Lesser Shennongjia. The golden monkey (Rhinopithecus roxellana) population, Chinese dove trees and other rare trees, as well as forests ecological system are protected. Shennong Stream, a tributary of Yangtze River, rises in the southern slopes of Shennongjia. With a length of 60 kilometers, it zigzags its way southward among deep valleys. After collecting water of more than 20 streams and waterfalls, the stream empties in the surging Yangtze River at last. Drifting down stream with the river is

the most wonderful travel style. Here, the water of stream is crystal clear, the rocky and wooded cliffs rise steeply on both sides of the narrow river, the air is full of fragrance of flowers and wild monkeys play leisurely. On the boat, one would feel that he is in a beautiful and poetic painted gallery and seeks tranquility of soul.

Wudang Mountain: Originally known as Taihe (Supreme Harmony), the Wudang Mountain is located southwest of Danjiangkou City in Hubei Province, facing the Danjiangkou Reservoir and backing onto the forest of Shennongjia. It stretches imposing more than 400 kilometers. Within an area of 240 square kilometers, there are 72 peaks, 36 rocks, 24 streams and 9 springs. Dotted with magical caves and covered with luxuriant trees, the scenic area looks so spectacular. The major peak, Tianzhu (Heavenly Pillar), stands 1,612 meters high, and what's surprise is that all other peaks lean toward the Tianzhu. With the amazing and marvelous natural scenery, the Wudang Mountain has long been known for its traditional Taoist culture. It is a famous Taoist mountain and the birthplace of Wudang Martial Arts. It is believed that Zhenwu Great Emperor, a Taoist patron saint, attained the Way here. Atop on the mountain are cultural and historical sites of different dynasties, as well as the majestic and solemn Taoist architectural complex built in the Ming Dynasty (1368-1644), which was inscribed on the World Heritage List in 1994. Major tourist spots include Jindian (Golden Hall), Zixiaogong (Palace of Purple Heaven), Yuanheguan (Taoist Monastery of Primary Harmony) and Nanyan (South Rock).

Xiling Gorge: Located in Yichang City of Hubei Province, the Xiling Gorge is the longest and most beautiful among the Three Gorges of the Yangtze River. The 76-kilometer- long section stretching from Nanjinguan Pass of Yichang City in the east to Xikou in Zigui County features a great number of shoals and torrents, and it is widely known as the Gate of Hell. Sandwiched by lofty peaks and jagged rocks of grotesque shapes, the gorge boasts such attractions as Bingshubaojianxia (Gorge of Book on the Art of War and Precious Sword), Niuganmafeixia (Gorge of Ox's Liver and Horse's Lung), Huangniuxia (Ox Gorge), Dengyingxia (Gorge of Lamp's Shadow), Qingtan (Blue Shoal), Xietan (Releasing Shoal), Konglingtan (Kongling Ridge Shoal), as well as relics of rock coffins of ancient Ba People, Sanyoudong (Three-Travel Cave), Luyouquan (Lu You Spring), and so on. Stand-

ing on the riverbank, four grotesque rocks rise in the shapes of the four legendary figures in *Journey to the West*, a famous classic Chinese novel describing four monks in the Tang Dynasty (618-907) whose adventures take them west to India. The four lifelike figures appear — Monkey King (Sun Wukong) shading his eyes with his hand, Pigsy (Zhu Bajie) sticking out his pot belly, Monk Sandy (Sha Heshang) striding vigorously shouldered burdens and Monk Xuanzang putting his palms together.

Songshan Mountain Scenic Resort: Located in Dengfeng City of Henan Province, Songshan Mountain is called the Central Mountain of the Five Sacred Mountains, and has been granted the titles of "National Important Scenic Resort" and "National Geological Park". The Songshan featuring precipitousness is composed of Taishi (Great Palace) and Shaoshi (Lesser Palace) mountains, which stretch about 100 kilometers and include 72 peaks. Junjifeng (Steep Supremacy Peak) is the main peak of the Songshan with an elevation of nearly 1,500 meters. The Songshan has peaks rising one higher than another, sheer precipices, luxuriant trees, and has been famed for "Eight Grand Views" and "Twelve Attractions" since ancient times. Additionally, it is known throughout the world as the cradle of Shaolin Kong-fu (martial arts). The mountain also boasts a large number of cultural relics, the most famous among which include Shaolin Temple nicknamed the Number One Temple under Heaven; Songyuesi brick pagoda, the earliest of its kind extant in China; Sputa Forest in Shaolin Temple, the largest group of tomb-pagoda in China Songyang Academy, one of the most famous academies in ancient China, and so on.

Sanqing Mountain: About 50 kilometers north of Yushan County in Jiangxi Province, Sanqing Mountain is reputed as the "First Fairy Mount of South China". Yujingfeng (Peak of Jade Capital), its main peak, rises to 1,817 meters above sea level. Three high peaks — Yujing, Yuhua (Jade Flower) and Yuxu (Jade Void) — stand resembling the three gods worshipped in Taoism (Taoist Trinity), hence the name. And it is a Taoist holy land. Covering a total area of 220 square kilometers, the Sanqing Mountain scenic area boasts 48 peaks, nearly 100 grotesque rocks and gorgeous

views. The fantastic peaks, odd shaped rocks, green pines, ancient trees, mysterious clouds, magic halo, cascading waterfalls and gushing springs together constitute its charming scenery, which features the precipitous east part, the wonderful west part, the graceful north part, the unrivalled beautiful south part and the imposing middle part. The imposing peaks come in a variety of shapes and are all natural works of art. There are many scenic spots of different interests, of which the peaks of Guanyintingqu (Avalokitesvara Bodhisattva Enjoying the Music), Sichunushen (Goddess of Spring) and Jumangchushan (Gigantic Boa) are collectively known as the "Three Wonders of Sanqing Mountain".

Seven-Star Crags Scenic Area: Lying in the northern suburbs of Zhaoqing, 4 kilometers from the city proper, the area covers an area of 8 square kilometers and is composed of the Xinghu (Star Lake) and seven razor-sharp monoliths. It has been famous for its "perilous cliffs, queer shaped rocks, fascinating caves and ancient temples". The lake features limpid waves and misty scene, and seven wooded crags — Langfeng (Spacious Wind), Yuping (Jade Screen), Shishi (Stone Room), Tianzhu (Heavenly Pillar), Chanchu (Toad), Xianzhang (Celestial Palm) and Apo (Old Woman) — stand by the lake in various shapes, resemble the Big Dipper in the firmament, hence the name. The graceful crags are encircled by a vast expanse of lovely waters, the long dike zigzags its way, and each of the ancient caves has its own different characteristics. All these form a typical of the South China landscape, inducing fantastic reveries. The picturesque scenery wins it the reputation of "Owning both the limestone peaks in Guilin and the water of West Lake in Hangzhou". The 80-odd scenic spots include 7 crags, 8 caves, 5 lakes and 6 ridges.

Dinghu Mountain Nature Reserve: About 18 kilometers northeast of Zhaoqing City of Guangdong Province, the Dinghu Mountain ranks the first among the Four Most Famous Mountains in south of the Five Ridges. There is a lake on the top of mountains, so the mountain was called Dinghu (Top Lake), and then it was misspelled as the Tripod Lake, which has the same sound but written with different homophonic characters. But legend has it that Emperor Huangdi once cast a tripod here, hence the name. The Dinghu Mountain Nature Reserve consists of more than 10 peaks including Dinghu, Sanbao (Three Treasures), Fenglai (Phoenix Coming) and Jilong (Chicken Coop), among which Jilong Peak is the highest in Zhujiang

(Pearl River) Delta with an elevation of about 1,000 meters and has such types of vegetation as valley rain forest, subtropics monsoon evergreen broadleaf forest, subtropics broadleaf forest, and others. Due to its dense primeval forests and unique research value, the Dinghu Mountain Nature Reserve is reputed as a "Storehouse of Gene" and "Living Natural Museum". Additionally, since the whole Tropic of Cancer is mainly deserts and dry grassland except the Dinghu Mountain, it is also known as the "Emerald of the Tropic of Cancer" and was listed into the Man and Nature Biosphere by the UNESCO.

Xiqiao Mountain Nature Reserve: About 68 kilometers from Guangzhou, the Xiqiao Mountain in southwest Nanhai District of Foshan City in Guangdong Province is reputed as a Bright Pearl in Zhujiang Delta. Covering a total area of 14 square kilometers, the mountain area comprises 72 peaks, 36 caves and 28 waterfalls. An extinct volcano, Xiqiao Mountain is widely regarded as the place to appreciate the mountain's natural beauty and features steep and grotesque peaks, secluded and mysterious caves, torrential waterfalls and streams, mirror-like lakes and pools and abundant woodland. Since the ancient times, it has been one of the two most beautiful mountains in the south of Guangdong. During the Qing Dynasty, the Xiqiao Yunpu (Cloud-like Waterfall on the Xiqiao Mountain) was listed as one of the Eight Grand View of Guangzhou. The picturesque scenery, sweet voice of the nature and touching folklores lure countless painters and poets seeking tranquility and inspiration, leaving numerous famous paintings and poems.

Dongjiao Coconut Forest: Hainan Province is located at the southernmost tip of China, facing Guangdong Province across the Qiongzhou Strait. The second largest island of China, Hainan features beautiful views and pleasant weather and is known throughout the world for its tropical scenery. A vast expanse of sea, charming landscape, radiant and enchanting sun light, pure and blue sky, gold sand beach, verdant forest of coconut trees, as well as gentle sea wind, capture visitors' dreamlike imagination. The Dongjiao Coconut Forest, nicknamed the Great Wall of Coconut Forest, has 500,000 coconut trees of various varieties of coconut species including green coco, red coco, tall coco, water coco, and so on. It is one of the Top Ten Seashores in China, and an outstanding representative of Hainan's tropical scenery. A local saying goes: "The output of coconut in Wenchang makes up roughly 50

per cent of the total of the province, while Dongjiao's coconut forest ranks the first in Wenchang." In this holiday resort, when a wind comes up, ten-*li* of coconut forest swings with the wind, like continuous green waves and also resembling sweet and charming dancing girls.

Nanwan Monkey Island: Located in Lingshui Li Autonomous County, the Nanwan Monkey Island is actually a narrow peninsula lying in the bay. Facing the sea on three sides, it covers an area of about 10 square kilometers. With luxuriant and ever-green vegetation, dense brushwood, rocks and caves, as well as abundant fruit trees including coconut, leechee, jack-fruit and carambola, this is a unique site that provides a refuge for monkeys. In 1965, a nature monkey reserve was established on the island. More than 1,000 monkeys inhabit the area. Visitors are treated to sight of monkeys frolicking and playing with each other, making a trip to this island a wonderful experience. Beyond the monkeys as the dominant species, the peninsula is also home to 400 species of tropical plants, nearly 20 species of animals such as red deer, otter and Manis pentadactyla, almost 30 species of birds including Chinese francolin and Upupa epops Hoopoe and such reptile class animal as boa and lizard.

Detian Waterfall: The Detian Waterfall is located in Daxin County, which is under the jurisdiction of Chongzuo City of Guangxi Zhuang Autonomous Region. Connecting with the Ban Gioc Waterfall of Viet Nam, it is the largest transnational waterfall in Asia and the second in the world. The waterfall takes its source from the Guichun River, which rises in Jingxi County of Guangxi, flows into Viet Nam and returns back to Guangxi. The upper reaches of the waterfall twisting and turning, meets a breakdown of the riverbed. Then the water rushes down a three-tiered cliff with tremendous force, forming a fantastic landscape. The spectacular waterfall is about 200 meters wide with a drop of over 70 meters during the flood season, like a huge silver curtain hanging on the cliff. The waterfall gives out a deafening sound of the roaring, which could be heard several kilometers away. It is particularly superb when rainbows arch from the plunge pool of the waterfall under the shining sun.

武陵源风景名胜区
Wulingyuan Scenic Area

武陵源风景名胜区位于湖南省西北部武陵山脉中，由张家界国家森林公园、索溪峪和天子山三大各具特色的风景区组成，整体宏大，景观丰富，以奇峰、怪石、幽谷、秀水、溶洞"五绝"闻名于世。景区内到处是奇峻的山峰、茂密的森林、纵横的沟壑、密布的溪洞、变幻的烟云、珍禽异兽和醉人的田园风光，构成一幅立体画卷，蔚为壮观。

武陵源有峰峦3100余座，高低参差，千姿百态。这里的峰石与别处不同，直立而密集，举目四望，如剑如笋，直指青天；似人似兽，变化万千，带给游人无尽的想像空间。突兀入眼的岩壁、峰石，配上青松、红枫，俨然一座天然盆景，堪称天下奇观。

武陵源又有"秀水八百"之称，众多的瀑、泉、溪、潭、湖，多姿多彩，各呈其妙。其中，金鞭溪全长5.7千米，穿行在峭峰幽谷之间，溪水清澈，腾宕多姿，将沿途众多自然风景穿成一串，溪畔花草鲜美，鸟鸣山幽，人行其中，犹在画中游。

武陵源的溶洞数量多、规模大，极富特色，有名可数的就有黄龙洞、观音洞、响水洞、龟栖洞、飞云洞和金螺洞等。其中，黄龙洞全长7.5千米，分为四层，洞内既有水又有山，遍布造型奇特的石笋、石柱、石瀑、石树、石帘、石花、石盆……被称为"洞穴学研究的宝库"，是武陵源最为著名的游览胜地。

武陵源地区气候温和多雨，无酷暑严寒。这里拥有成片的原始次生林，森林覆盖率达85%，珙桐、银杏、水杉、龙虾花等奇花珍木漫山遍野，猕猴、灵猫、角雉、锦鸡等珍禽异兽出没其间，使它成为资源丰富的绿色植物宝库和野生动物乐园。

与优美的自然风光相映成趣的是武陵源的田园风光。这里是土家族、白族、苗族等少数民族的聚居地。在如屏如画的峰峦环抱中，块块梯田、座座村宅点缀其间，山青水绿，炊烟袅袅，好一处淡雅宁静的天上人间！

1992年，联合国教科文组织将武陵源风景名胜区列为世界自然遗产项目。主要旅游景点有天子山、黄狮寨、金鞭溪、宝峰湖、黄龙洞、十里画廊等。

The Wulingyuan Scenic Area spreads out among the Wulingyuan Mountains in the northwest of Hunan province, and consists of three parts — Zhangjiajie National Park, Suoxiyu Nature Reserve and Tianzi Mountain Nature Reserve — possessing different characteristics. Featuring five wonders of marvelous peaks, incredible rock formations, tranquil valleys, beautiful water and magical karst caves, the scenic area presents a unique landscape of high and precipitous mountains, luxuriant plants and trees, deep gorges, crisscross streams, ever-changing clouds and mist, rare birds and animals, as well as intoxicating idyll.

The Wulingyuan Scenic Area boasts some 3,100 peaks, spectacular and grotesque, lofty and elegant. They stand intensively, some look like swords or bamboo shoots, while some resemble figures or animals, simply beyond one's imagination. The peaks and rocks, dotted with green pines and red maples, form a huge natural potted landscape.

Wulingyuan is wonderful for its water attractions. There are breathtaking waterfalls, fascinating lakes, dribbling streams, calm pools and picturesque brooks. It is said 800 graceful streams lace among the valleys, of which, the Jinbianxi (Golden Whip Brook) is the most famous. Lengthening 5.7 kilometers, the brook winds its way between steep peaks and secluded gorges, threading many scenic spots. On both sides are green grass and fragrant flowers. Walking along it, visitors have a feeling of rambling in a picture.

Numerous limestone caves also add charms to the Wulingyuan Scenic Area, such as Huanglongdong (Yellow Dragon Cave), Guanyindong (Avalokitesvara's Cave), Xiangshuidong (Noisy Water Cave), Guiqidong (Dwelling Turtle Cave), Feiyundong (Flying Clouds Cave), Jinluodong (Golden Conch Cave) and so on. Huanglongdong, 7,500 meters long, consists of four stories. It is treasure house for various gestured calcium carbonate deposits, including stone bamboo shoots, stone pillars, stone waterfalls, stone trees, stone curtains, stone flowers, stone basins, etc., and to your surprise, it houses hills and lakes. The Huanglongdong is one of most celebrated attractions in Wulingyuan.

The area is rich in flora and fauna for the mild and rainy climate. In dense forests covering over 85 per cent of the scenic area grow rare species of trees including Chinese dove tree, ginkgo, metasequoia and lobster flower, and inhabited by such rare species of birds and animals as macaque, civet, tragopan and golden pheasant. It is reputed as the "treasury of green plants" and "paradise of wild animals".

The beautiful natural scenery is skillfully borrowed to enhance the beauty of the rural landscape. Since the ancient times, people of Tujia, Bai, Miao and other ethnic minorities have lived here. Screened by picturesque, wooded peaks and spotted with terraced fields and village houses, the land is a heaven on earth.

In 1992, the Wulingyuan became a world natural heritage site of the UNESCO. Major attractions include Tianzishan (Mountain of Heavenly Son), Huangshizhai (Mountain of Yellow Lion's Stockaded Village), Jinbianxi, Baofenghu (Lake of Precious Peak), Huanglongdong and Shilihualang (Ten-*Li* Gallery).

湖南省張家界天子山雪景
Tianzi Mountain of Zhangjiajie after
Snow, Hunan Province

湖南省张家界风光
Misty Scene of Zhangjiajie,
Hunan Province

湖南省张家界黄狮寨冬景
Snow Scene of Huangshizhai (Yellow-Lion
Camp) of Zhangjiajie, Hunan Province

湖南省衡山风光
Beautiful Scenery of the Hengshan Mountain, Hunan Province

1. 湖北省长江西陵峡
Xiling Gorge of the Yangtze River,
Hubei Province

2. 湖北省神农架风景区：神农溪
Shennong Stream of the Shennongjia
Scenic Area, Hubei Province

3. 湖北省武当山风景名胜区
Wudang Mountain Scenic Area,
Hubei Province

1. 湖北省武当山风景名胜区
   Wudang Mountain Scenic Area,
   Hubei Province

2. 河南省嵩山风景名胜嵩岳寺塔
   Dagoba in the Songyue Temple of the
   Songshan Mountain Scenic Resort,
   Henan Province

3. 河南省嵩山风景名胜区石淙河
   Shicong River in the Songshan
   Mountain Scenic Resort, Henan

1.江西省流坑村乡间景色
  Rustic Scene of Liukeng Village,
  Jiangxi Province

2.3.江西省三清山风景区
  Sanqing Mountain Scenic Resort,
  Jiangxi Province

庐山风景名胜区
Lushan Mountain Scenic Area

庐山风景名胜区位于江西省北部，雄踞于长江之北，东濒中国最大的淡水湖——鄱阳湖。庐山是中国风景名山之一和著名的避暑胜地，拥有雄奇的山峰，变幻的云海，神奇的飞瀑，宜人的气候，以及历史悠久的文化古迹。

庐山共由99座山峰组成，其中，主峰大汉阳峰海拔1474米。1996年，庐山被联合国教科文组织列入《世界遗产名录》。主要风景名胜有五老峰、三叠泉、含鄱口、三宝树、龙首崖、大小天池、花径、东林寺、白鹿书院等。

庐山具有突出价值的地质、地貌和独特的第四纪冰川遗迹，奇峦秀色，驰誉天下。景区内层峦叠嶂，陡峭挺拔，群峰灵秀，异石突兀，最著名的有大汉阳峰、五老峰、含鄱岭等。最高峰大汉阳峰崔巍而立，据说，因站在峰巅之上可观汉阳灯火而得名。五老峰为五座山峰，仰望形如五位老翁席地而坐，故人们把这原出于一山的五个山峰统称为"五老峰"。五座山峰，若接霄汉，危松虬立，传说唐代大诗人李白曾在此隐居。含鄱口海拔近1300米，与群峰绵延相连，形成一个巨大壑口，势如一口汲尽山麓的鄱阳湖，故得名。山巅是观赏旭日东升的绝佳胜地。

由于傍依江湖，庐山上云雾缭绕，云海奇观引人入胜。北宋文学家苏东坡曾写下"不识庐山真面目，只缘身在此山中"的著名诗句。位于大天池西南侧的龙首崖便是观赏云海的好去处。龙首崖悬壁峭立，一石横亘其上，宛如苍龙昂首，崖边几棵虬松，恰似龙须，故名。每当大雾袭来，顷刻之间，整个庐山似被淹没在茫茫云海之中，煞是壮观。云雾时而汹涌澎湃如奔腾江河，时而轻飘曼舞如涓涓细流。游客站在崖上，有如乘龙上天入海，出入仙境。

庐山之美，瀑布居首。庐山之上共有22处飞瀑，这其中又以三叠泉为最美。三叠泉位于庐山以东的九叠谷中，瀑布从五老峰奔泻而下，依山势分为上、中、下三级，落差150余米，被誉为"庐山第一奇观"，有"未到三叠泉，不算庐山客"之说。

庐山自古以来就以其秀丽的风景为诸多文人雅士所景仰，并留下了4000余首颂扬它的诗词文赋，许多为脍炙人口的名篇。

Located in the northern part of Jiangxi Province, Lushan Mountain faces the Yangtze River to the north and borders on the east with the largest fresh water lake in China, Poyang Lake. With this fantastic blend of magnificent peaks and cragged cliffs, wonderful flying waterfalls, historical sites, as well as ever-changing sea of clouds and a warm and mild climate, it is one of China's best summer resorts and tourist attractions. The mountain consists of 99 peaks, the tallest being Dahanyang, rising to the height of 1,474 meters above sea level. It became a world heritage site of the UNESCO in 1996. The main scenic spots on the mountain include Wulaofeng (Peak of the Five Old Men), Sandiequan (Three-Tier Spring), Hanpokou (Pass Containing Poyang Lake), Sanbaoshu (Three-Treasure Tree), Longshouya (Dragon-Head Cliff), Great and Lesser Tianchi (Heavenly Lake), Huajing (Flower Path), Donglinsi (Temple of East Forest) and Bailu Shuyuan (White-Deer Cave Academy).

Lushan Mountain is a fault mountain formed in the Quaternary Period. As a result of tremendous rubbing and grinding of glaciers, its grotesque and rolling peaks, cragged cliffs look all the more precipitous, making the mountain even more mysterious. The most famous peaks include Dahanyang, Wulaofeng and Hanpoling (Ridge of Containing Poyang Lake). Being the highest peak, Dahanyang stands tall and imposing. The summit of the peak provides a general view of Hanyang, hence the name. The Wulaofeng is a collective name of five peaks resembling five old men who sit shoulder by shoulder. They are known for the sturdy and strange-looking pines. It was said that Li Bai, a great poet of the Tang Dynasty, once lived here in seclusion. Rising to nearly 1,300 meters above sea level, the Hanpoling links with other undulating peaks, and forms a huge ravine mouth containing the Poyang Lake. From the top of mountain pass overlooking the vast and misty Poyang Lake, visitors can see the junk-dotted lake blending with the sky and enjoy the spectacular scene of sun-rising.

Thanks to its location close to lake and river, Lushan Mountain is celebrated throughout the world for its impressive sea of clouds. The enveloping clouds and mists make it very hard to define the true shapes of the billowing peaks and ridges. Su Dongpo, a well-known poet of the Northern Song Dynasty, described it in one of his famous poets: "The failure to get the real looks of the mountain only results in the fact that you are right in the midst of it." The Longshouya is an ideal place that appreciated the unforgettable marvelous spectacle. Springing up some thousand feet out of the ground, the cliff rears in the sky like a dragon head, with a few winding pine trees resembling the dragon's beards. When the whole mountain lost in the cloud and mist, no one could tell the true shape of Lushan. The sea of clouds changes in shapes: now like a river with turbulent waves, and now like a murmur stream, bestowing the mountain endless enchantment of mysteriousness and beauty. Standing on the cliff, the tourists could feel like riding a huge dragon and coming to the wonderland.

The Lushan is also famous for it 22 waterfalls, of which the Sandiequan is especially outstanding, and reputed as the "First Wonder of Lushan". Situated in Jiudie (Nine-Fold) Valley, east of Lushan, the Sandiequan plummets more than 150 meters from the pinnacle of the Wulaofeng and comes to an abrupt end against the three-tiered rocks at the cliffs base creating a spectacular screen of mist. A famous saying goes "He who hasn't been to the Three-Tier Spring is not a real visitor to the Lushan".

Lushan's beauty has been admired for centuries. A lot of poets and scholars had traveled around the mountain and left a great deal of praise, many of which enjoy great popularity.

江西省庐山风景名胜区
**Lushan Mountain Scenic Area,
Jiangxi Province**

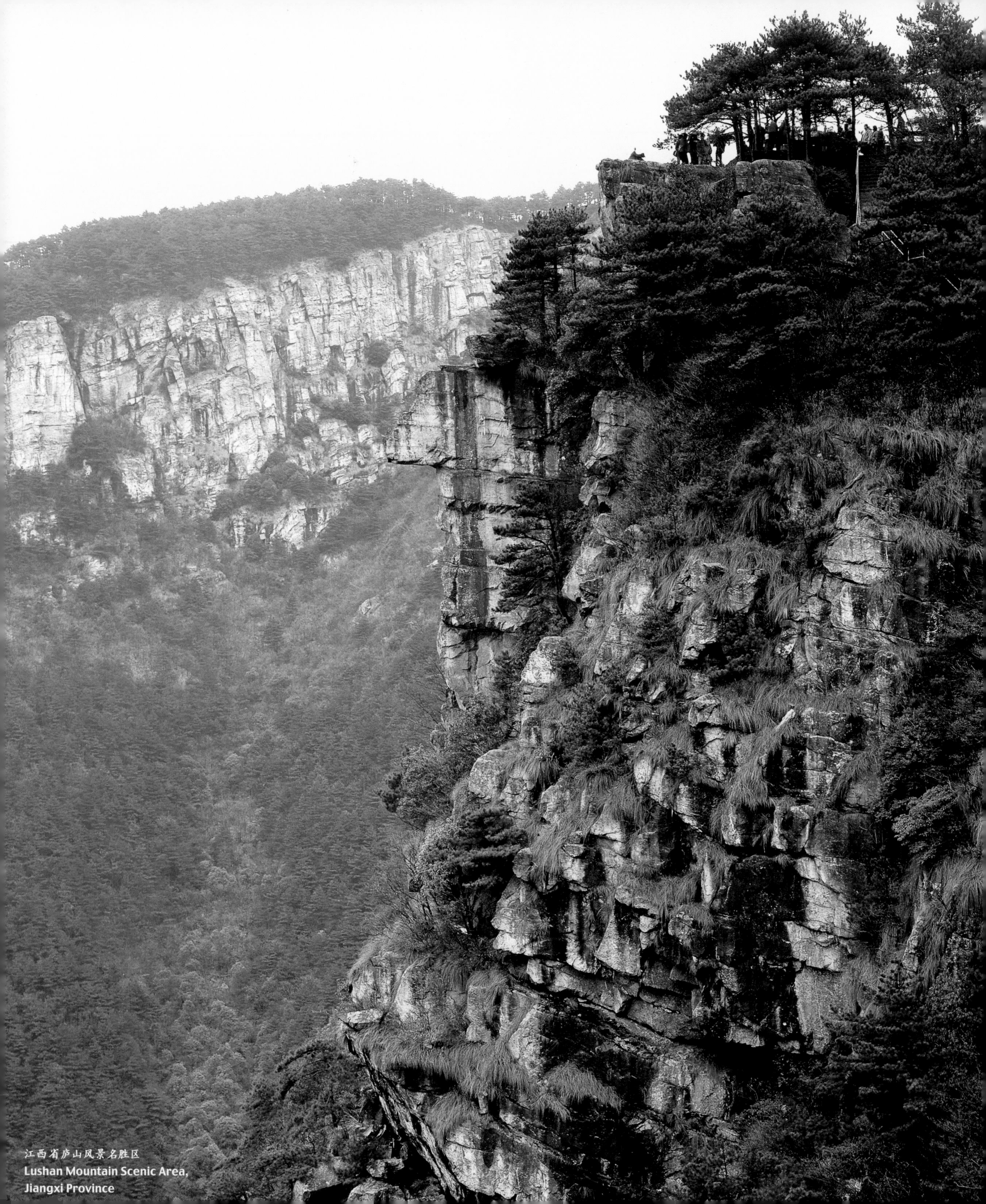

江西省庐山风景名胜区
Lushan Mountain Scenic Area,
Jiangxi Province

江西省婺源县秋色
Wuyuan County in Autumn,
Jiangxi Province

广东省鼎湖山瀑布
Waterfall in the Dinghu Mountain
Nature Reserve, Guangdong Province

广东省七星岩风景区
Seven-Star Crags Scenic Area,
Guangdong Province

1. 广东省西樵山风景名胜区
Xiqiao Mountain Nature Reserve,
Guangdong Province

2. 广东省丹霞山风景区
Danxia Mountain Scenic Area,
Guangdong Province

3. 海南省南湾猴岛一景
A View of Nanwan Monkey Island,
Hainan Province

4. 海南省东山岭奇岩怪石
Oddly Shaped Rocks on the
Dongshanling (East Mountain
Range), Hainan Province

海南省东郊椰林南国风光
**Attractive Scenery of Dongjiao Coconut
Forest, Hainan Province**

海南省陵水椰岛
Coconut Island in Lingshui Li
Autonomous County, Hainan Province

海南省第一大河万泉河
The Largest River of Hainan Province:
Wanquan (Ten-Thousand Springs) River

桂林山水
Landscape in Guilin

广西壮族自治区地形略成盆地状，石灰岩分布区约占全自治区总面积的一半。因高温多雨，溶蚀成千姿百态的峰林、岩洞，漓江像一条青绸绿带，盘绕其间，共同组成了如梦如幻的山水胜景，这也是广西最引为骄傲的旅游资源。

漓江发源于兴安县的猫儿山，全长437千米。奇峰夹岸，碧水萦回，山光水影，景色十分秀美。位于漓江之畔的桂林市，是一座著名的风景旅游城市和历史文化名城，其境内的漓江流域是广西喀斯特岩溶峰林地貌的代表之作。尤其是从桂林到阳朔这一段83千米的水程，岩溶景观奇特壮丽，山水风光别具一格，堪称漓江风景区的精华。游览区景因时变，步移景换，即便天气不同，其神韵也大不相同：晴可观青峰万点，秀水千曲；阴可赏轻纱笼罩，群峰忽隐忽现；雨可看水波浩淼，烟岚迷离……幻化无穷，宛若人间仙境，千百年来不知醉倒了多少文人墨客。山秀、水清、岩奇、石美，桂林因此享有"山水甲天下"的美誉。

桂林市内最有代表性的景点主要有：象鼻山、伏波山、叠彩山、七星公园和芦笛岩等。其中，象鼻山是桂林山水的象征，也是桂林市的标志，位于漓江西滨，山形酷似一头伸鼻吸水的巨象，因此得名。"象鼻"与"象腿"之间形成水月洞，每逢月朗之夜，水月洞倒影如一轮皎月浮江，与南望的穿山月岩远近相映，构成"漓江双月"的绝妙意境。

桂林周边县城的风光同样秀丽迷人。从桂林到阳朔，漓江两岸美景，处处皆是，如风景画廊，主要景点有月岩、冠岩、秀山、浪石奇景、螺狮山、碧莲峰、书童山等。阳朔境内民风古朴，翠竹、茂林、田野、山庄、渔村随处可见，田园风光如诗如画，使人赏心悦目，犹入世外桃源，有"阳朔山水甲桂林"的盛誉。兴坪更是漓江风景线的高潮部分，荟萃了漓江山水风光的精华。放眼四望，青峰叠翠，江水迂回，一步十景，景景相接，美不胜收。许多优秀的美术作品都诞生在这里，中国著名画家徐悲鸿在这里写生时，曾评价"阳朔美景在兴坪"。

The terrain of Guangxi Zhuang Autonomous Region is shaped like a basin, and more than half of it is covered with limestone. High temperatures and abundant rainfall have corroded the limestone into a forest of ridges, peaks and caves, making Guangxi a famous tourist attraction with the green hills and pellucid, zigzag belt-like Lijiang River setting off each other.

The Lijiang River has its source in the Maor (Kitten) Mountain in Xing'an County, lengthening about 437 kilometers, and gorgeous Karst peaks on its both sides give you surprises at each bend under the blue sky. The scenery in Guilin is the most typical and most charming. Guilin is an ancient and beautiful city on the shore of the mesmerizing Lijiang River in northeastern Guangxi. The landscape along the limpid river in Guilin's territory is an outstanding representative of Guangxi's Karst landform, and a golden strand of scenic wonder meanders from Guilin to Yangshuo, a spanning of 83 kilometers, where rivers passes an endless procession of distinct peaks covered by luxuriant vegetation and stunning scenic spots are everywhere on both sides. The beauty of Lijiang River lies in a lingering charm that survives the charge of seasons throughout a year, of hours in a day and of different weather, and scenes change with each pace. In clear days, the limpid river looks like a green ribbon, and the riverside hills are as blue as jade hairpins; in cloudy days, peaks tucked away in the woods or positioned abreast at the waterfront appear indistinctly in gauze-like haze; while in rainy days, mists and waves stretch far into the distance… What a wonderland in man's world! The serene mountains, sparkling waters, and exotic rocks typical of the karst landmass of the city have inspired the saying: "The landscape of Guilin is unmatched under Heaven."

Within the city of Guilin, representative scenic spots are: Xiangbishan (Elephant-Trunk Hill), Fuboshan (Wave Subduing Hill), Diecaishan (Folded Brocade Hill), Qixing (Seven-Star) Park and Ludiyan (Reed Flute Cave). Of them, the Xiangbishan situated majestically on the western bank of Lijiang River is supposed to be the logo of Guilin landscape, as well as the landmark of the city. The hill resembles an elephant sucking water from the river with its long trunk, hence the name. Under the hill, there is a "water-moon cave" which separates the truck and its body. The most impressive is said to be the water reflection of this cave when the moonlight sprinkles over the river, and along with the reflection of a round hole through the Chuanshan which is known as Yueyan (Moon-Like Cave), it is the famous scenic spot named Double Moons on the Lijiang River.

Guilin's scenery is the best in the world, and the scenery in its surrounding counties is also beautiful. Cruising by boat on the Lijiang River is like entering a picture gallery. There are many scenic spots from Guilin to Yangshuo, including Yueyan, Langshi Qijing (Wonderful View of Rocks in Waves), Luoshishan (Spiral Shell Hill), Bilianfeng (Green Lotus Peak), Shutongshan (Page Boy Hill), and others. Yangshuo County is well known in the world for its striking mountain-and-river rural scenery. Within the territory, the rural scenery is as beautiful as a painting, and the folkway here is simple. Pinnacled peaks pop up and surprise visitors at each bend of the river, and green bamboos, luxuriant woods, fields, countryside houses and fishing villages are everywhere. All these create an idyllic and beautiful scene of the life removed from concrete cities. Hence the saying: "The landscape of Yangshuo is unmatched in Guilin." The river takes a big turn at Xingping, where, endowed with beautiful and poetic scenery, is the climax of the Lijiang and has been reproduced in many Chinese landscape paintings. Xu Beihong (1895-1953), a famous painter and excellent educator of fine arts in China, once said that the most impressive and stunning view of Yangshou was in Xingping.

广西壮族自治区桂林山水
Landscape in Guilin City,
Guangxi Zhuang Autonomous Region

1. 广西壮族自治区桂林山水
   Landscape in Guilin City, Guangxi Zhuang Autonomous Region

2. 广西壮族自治区阳朔高田风光
   Scenery of Gaotian Town, Yangshuo County, Guangxi Zhuang Autonomous Region

3. 广西壮族自治区桂林晨曦
   First Light of a Day, Guilin, Guangxi Zhuang Autonomous Region

广西壮族自治区乡村一景
Rustic Scene of Guangxi
Zhuang Autonomous Region

广西壮族自治区德天瀑布
**Detian Waterfall, Guangxi
Zhuang Autonomous Region**

广西壮族自治区北部湾风光
**North Bay, Guangxi Zhuang
Autonomous Region**

台湾省日月潭风光
**Scenery of Riyue (Sun and Moon)
Pool, Taiwan Province**

West China

美丽的中国·西部

四川省 Sichuan Province

重庆市 Chongqing Municipality

贵州省 Guizhou Province

云南省 Yunnan Province

西藏自治区 Tibet Autonomous Region

陕西省 Shaanxi Province

甘肃省 Gansu Province

青海省 Qinghai Province

宁夏回族自治区 Ningxia Hui Autonomous Region

新疆维吾尔自治区 Xinjiang Uygur Autonomous Region

中国西部主要旅游景区简介：

瞿塘峡：我国第一大河——长江，全长6300千米，发源于青藏高原，奔流不息，流经四川盆地东缘时，犹如利剑开山劈岭，夺路向东浩荡流去，形成了壮丽雄奇、举世闻名的长江三峡，即瞿塘峡、巫峡和西陵峡。长江三峡西起重庆奉节县白帝城，东至湖北省宜昌市南津关，全长193千米，区内峭壁嵯峨，水流汹涌，风光奇绝，是世界著名的旅游景点。其中，瞿塘峡是三峡中最短最窄的峡谷，也是最险的一峡。瞿塘峡全长8千米，江面最宽处150米，最窄处仅50米。两岸绝壁对峙，状若两扇大门，长江之水奔腾澎湃，夺门直下，气势异常雄伟险峻。船行江中，仰望两岸，崖壁直立如墙，形成一线云天。

南温泉风景区：南温泉是重庆四大名泉之一，因位于重庆市南部，故名。泉水常温40摄氏度左右，适宜治疗风湿病口皮肤病，早在明代时就已开发利用。风景区距离市区约6千米，处于巴县山脉和涂山山脉的交汇处、花溪河畔，群山蜿蜒，峰峦叠翠，气候温和宜人，景观资源丰富，具有山、水、林、峡、洞等多种类型的自然景观。南温泉风景区内山峰峭立，林木秀美，泉流多姿，溶洞奇特，"虎啸悬流"、"弓桥泛月"等被誉为十二胜景。名胜多在花溪河沿岸，花溪河水从虎啸口流入南泉峡谷，本为涓涓细流，忽然洪流翻腾，飞泻而下，形成层层飞瀑，实为壮观。

峨眉山风景区：峨眉山坐落在四川盆地南部，距成都150千米，是中国佛教四大名山之一，传为普贤菩萨的道场。风景区面积300平方千米，主峰万佛顶海拔3099米。峨眉山风景区以优美的自然风光，悠久的佛教文化，丰富的动植物资源和独特的地质地貌而著称于世，被人们称为"仙山佛国"、"植物王国"、"动物乐园"、"地质博物馆"，有"峨眉天下秀"的美誉。金顶海拔3077米，以日出、云海、佛光、圣灯四大奇观最负盛名，其中，金顶云海尤为著名。晴朗之日，游客站在岩前，浩瀚无际的白云在岩下翻涌，千姿百态，瞬息万变，山峰犹如一座孤岛，在惊涛骇浪中时隐时现，煞是壮观。1996年，联合国教科文组织将其列入《世界遗产名录》。

黄龙风景名胜区：位于四川省阿坝藏族羌族自治州松潘县境内，因古老的黄龙寺而得名。风景区由黄龙、丹云霞、红星岩、雪宝顶和牟尼沟等景区组成，总面积1340平方千米。其雄奇的山岳、险峻的峡谷、绚丽的草原风光、浩瀚的林海、众多的湖泊以及丰富的动植物资源和独特的民族风情，展示出一幅幅神奇瑰丽的画卷，有"圣地仙境，人间瑶池"之美誉。黄龙沟为主景区，以高山、彩池、叠瀑及钙华景观令人叹为观止。沟底岩石晶莹光滑，随山势而失宕起伏、蜿蜒曲折，犹如一条黄龙盘旋而上，将大小彩池穿成一串美丽的项链。彩池形状各异，深浅不一，随着周围景色变化和阳光的反射角度不同，呈现出各种奇幻的颜色。1992年，黄龙风景名胜区被联合国教科文组织列为世界自然遗产项目。

四姑娘山风景区：位于四川省阿坝藏族羌族自治州小金县与汶川县交界处，由横断山脉中四座毗连的山峰组成。据当地藏民传说，这四座山峰是由四位美丽的少女化成，因此得名。四姑娘山以雄峻挺拔闻名，山体陡峭，常年积雪覆盖，云遮雾罩，冰清玉洁。最高一座峰海拔6250米，因四川最高峰——海拔7556米的贡嘎雪山被誉为"蜀山之王"，此座山峰又被称作"蜀山之后"。四姑娘山风景区东有岷江奔腾汹涌，西有"天险"大渡河咆哮不止，气候温和，雨量充沛，森林茂密，绿草如茵，风光极为秀美，颇具南欧神韵，因此又被喻为"东方的阿尔卑斯山"。景区主要由四姑娘山、巴郎山、双桥沟、长坪沟和海子沟等组成。其中，双桥沟全长约35千米，是四姑娘山最美的沟谷，有杨柳桥、五色山、猎人峰、鹰嘴岩、金鸡岭等诸多景点。置身其中，犹如进入了一个迷人的立体画廊，美景过目难忘。

青城山：位于四川省都江堰市西南，距成都66千米，是中国道教的发祥地之一。因山峰呈环形排列，状如城郭，又因山上林木葱茏，终年青翠，因此谓之青城山，以"青城天下幽"名扬四海。青城山山体主要由砾岩组成，最高峰海拔1600余米，分为前山和后山两大景区，有36峰、8大洞、72小洞、108景和11座道观之胜景，以及日出、云海、圣灯三大自然奇观。青城山还是中国四大道教名山，被称为"第五洞天"，道教创始人张道陵在此修炼并羽化，因此山上道教遗迹众多。青城山植被茂密，层峦叠翠，曲径通幽，古观藏趣，主要自然景观有千年银杏、金鞭岩、月城湖、朝阳洞、天然图画等。2000年，青城山和都江堰一起，被联合国教科文组织列入《世界遗产名录》。

卧龙自然保护区：位于四川省汶川县境内，地处青藏高原向四川盆地过渡地带的高山峡谷区，温暖湿润的气候环境，给森林植被的发育提供了优越条件，成为"活化石"大熊猫生存和繁衍后代的理想地区，被列为国家级自然保护区。保护区内峰峦叠嶂，云雾缭绕，地带性植被属亚热带常绿阔叶林，但随着海拔的升高，植被类型相应出现有规律的垂直变化，共有4000多种植物，其中包括珙桐、四川红杉、金钱槭、连香等多种珍贵种类，也为400多种动物的栖生提供了适宜的环境。除了大熊猫，这里还生活着金丝猴、羚牛、白唇鹿等50多种国家重点保护动物。卧龙以"熊猫之乡"、"宝贵的生物基因库"和"天然动植物园"的盛誉闻名中外。保护区内还有英雄沟、银厂沟等景区。雪山峡谷、原始森林、奇花异草、飞瀑流泉和悠闲漫步的大熊猫、攀援嬉戏的金丝猴、婉转轻歌的雀鸟……汇集成一种难以抗拒的诱人魅力，吸引着众多的中外游客和科学工作者前来观赏、探索。

梵净山：位于贵州省东北部铜仁地区江口、印江、松桃三县交界处，是武陵山脉的主峰，最高峰凤凰山海拔2572米。梵净山地貌和自然地理垂直分布很典型，这里群峰耸峙，层峦叠嶂，古木参天，森林茂密，是地球同纬度地带植物生态保护最完整的地区之一，被列为国家级自然保护区。梵净山有植物种类近3000种，其中有珙桐、钟萼木、铁杉、鹅掌楸等10多种国家重点保护植物，显示了植物区米成分的原始性和古老性，为全国罕见。梵净山还是珍异兽的乐园，有鸟类、两栖类和爬行类动物300多种，其中列为国家一、二、三类保护的珍稀动物就有17种，特别是黔金丝猴，目前世界上仅发现100多只。1986年，梵净山被纳入联合国教科文组织"世界人与生物圈自然保护区"。

黄果树瀑布：黄果树瀑布位于贵州省安顺市镇宁县西南白水河上，是贵州省最著名的景观之一。黄果树瀑布是中国第一大瀑布，享有"天下奇景"的美誉。白水河自东北向至黄果树地段时，因河床断裂，河水带着团团白雾倾泻而下，形成九级瀑布，气势磅礴，犹如万马奔腾。黄果树最大的瀑布宽约81米，落差70余米，激起的水珠可达90多米高，似银河倒泻，珠玑散空。瀑布对岸有观瀑亭，是观赏飞瀑壮丽景象的绝佳地点。在瀑布背面的悬崖中部，还有长约134米的水帘洞，迷离恍惚，若隐若现，宛如人间仙境。

玉龙雪山：玉龙雪山位于云南省丽江市坝子北15千米处，南北长35千米，东西宽约20千米。终年积雪的13座高峰由北向南横峙绵亘，在蔚蓝的天幕衬托下和云雾缭绕中宛如一条玉龙凌空飞舞，因此得名。13座山峰海拔均在4000米以上，其中，主峰扇子陡海拔5596米，是云南第二高峰。雪山上植物资源异常丰富，有"植物王国"之称种类繁多的植物按不同的气候带生长在不同的高度上，成为滇西北横断山脉植物的缩影。藏在雪山深处的云杉坪海拔3365米，雪峰拱卫，密林环绕，草甸平缓起伏，是纳西族神话传说中"玉龙第三国"的男女殉情处。

泸沽湖：位于云南省宁蒗彝族自治县和四川省盐源县交界处。湖面海拔2685米，总面积52平方千米，平均水深4米。泸沽湖四周青山环绕，森林茂密；湖区碧波荡漾，四季清澈；湖岛姿态各异，林木葱郁，风景醉人。泸沽湖不仅以风光秀丽著称于世，更以古老原始的民俗风情引人入胜。居住在湖畔的古老民族摩梭人，是纳西族的一支。他们至今保留着传统的母系社会形态，生活在以女性为轴心的大家庭里，拥有奇特而浪漫的走婚风俗，堪称人类母系社会的活化石，被誉为"现代女儿国"。

石林风景区：位于云南省石林彝族自治县境内，西距昆明84千米，总面积达350平方千米。这里有世界上著名的喀斯特岩溶地质奇观，为国家重点风景名胜区。据考证2.7亿年前，这里是汪洋大海，沉淀了巨厚层状石灰岩。经过地壳运动和造山运动，伸出海面，历经亿万年雨水和地下水的溶蚀和冲刷，形成这一奇特的地质景观。景区内群峰壁立，危石临空，参差错落，姿态各异；千千万万个石峰、石柱、石芽、石笋和石矛拔地而起，犹如一望无际

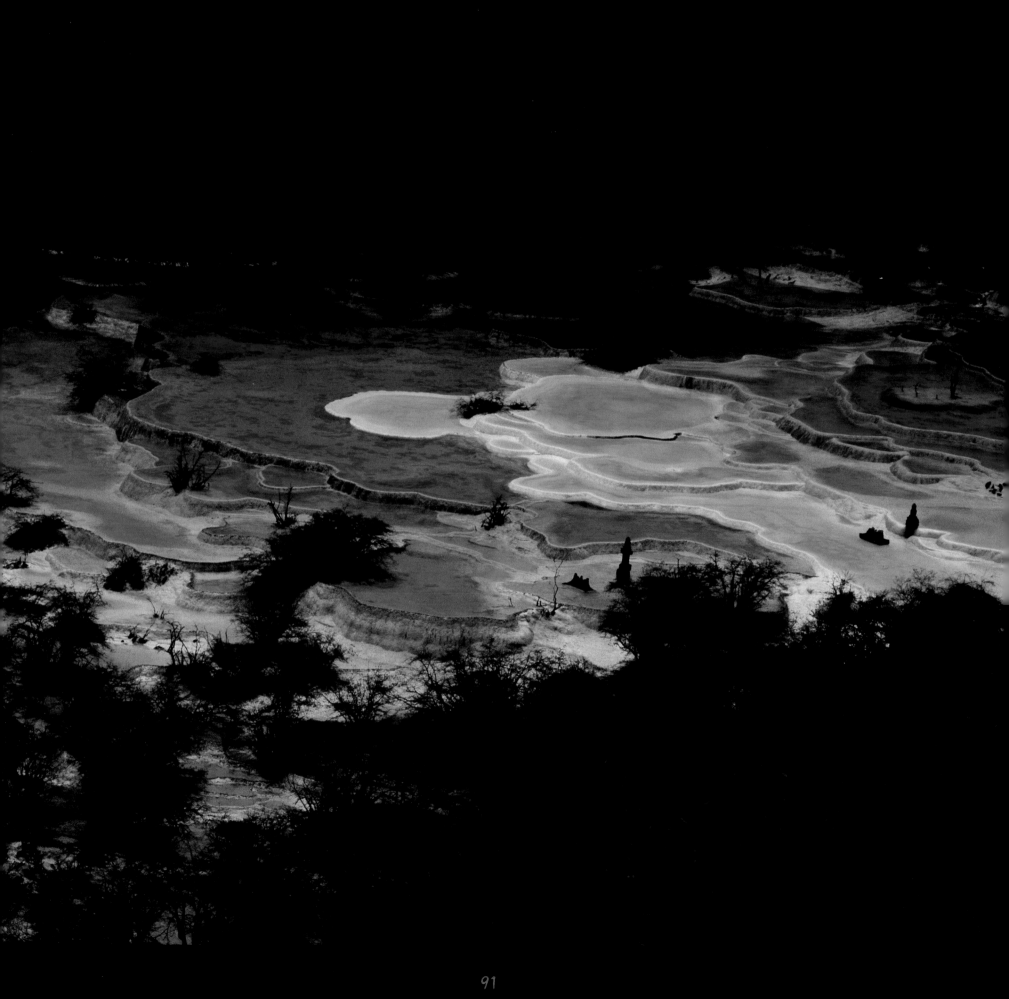

…松林，气势磅礴，被誉为"天下第一奇观"。整个风景区由大小石林、乃古石林、大叠水瀑布、月湖、芝云洞、地下石林和奇风洞等7个景区组成。

耳海：位于云南省大理市，海拔1980米，是一个风光秀美的高山湖泊，因形似人耳，风大浪急如海而得名。湖面积…50平方千米，是仅次于滇池的云南第二大湖。从坐落于湖畔西岸的苍山上俯瞰，洱海宛如一轮新月，自古以来被誉为"群山间的无瑕美玉"。湖水碧清，绿波鄰鄰，洁白…苍山霞雪倒映在湖中，被称作"银苍玉洱"奇观。然而，…引人入胜的莫过于洱海的月夜。每逢月圆之夜，明月高…青辉朗朗，湖中浮波光影，月圆如轮。天上月与海中…交相辉映，使游人宛入仙境，这便是胜景"洱海月"，与…关风、上关花和苍山雪构成大理风、花、雪、月四大美…

昆明滇池：昆明市位于云南中部，是云南省省会，四季如…，气候宜人，有"春城"之称。滇池坐落在西山脚下，以其绚丽迷人的风光，成为这座魅力都市中最吸引人的风景名胜之一。滇池，古称"昆明湖"、"滇南泽"，是云南…面积最大的高原湖泊，也是中国第六大淡水湖，海拔…885米，总面积300平方千米。湖泊位于群山环抱之中，…"高原明珠"的美称。这里终年树木常青，花开似锦；…区烟波浩渺，碧波荡漾；周围群峰竞秀，漫山苍翠；蓝…天白云之间，成群的红嘴鸥上下翻飞，自由盘旋；湖上渔…点点，水鸟翩翩。乘船出游，凉风习习，景色迷人，如…画中。

喜马拉雅山脉：西藏自治区位于我国西南边疆，为青藏高…的重要组成部分，平均海拔在4000米以上，被称为"世…屋脊"。唐古拉山绵延其北，喜马拉雅山耸立其南，东…横断山，西有昆仑山，中部有念青唐古拉山和冈底斯山，…共同构成了西藏独特的地理景观。其中，喜马拉雅山脉位…青藏高原西南边缘，山势高峻雄伟，连绵起伏2400多千…平均海拔高度达6000米以上，是世界上最雄伟高大而…最年轻的山系。地球上很少有地方能够比得上喜马拉雅…脉摄人心魄的壮丽景色。珠穆朗玛峰位于西藏定日县…、中国与尼泊尔交界处，海拔8844.43米，是世界最高…，被誉为"地球第三极"。山顶终年冰雪覆盖，冰川长…26千米，极为壮观。珠峰周围还环绕有30余座海拔在…000米以上的雪峰，其中，在我国境内海拔8000米以上…高峰还有：洛子峰（8516米）、马卡鲁峰（8463米）、卓…友峰（8201米）和希夏邦马峰（8012米）。广袤的大地，…杂的地貌，独特的高山高原自然风光和多样的气候，使…这一地区拥有强大的魅力，吸引着世界各地众多人们前来…观光、旅游、探险和考察。

华山：为五岳之西岳，位于关中平原东部陕西省华阴市南，…以险著称。奇峰耸立，绝壁巍峭，所以素有"自古华山一…条路"之誉。华山由落雁、朝阳、莲花、玉女和云台五座…峰组成。最高峰南峰落雁海拔2200米，因为归雁栖息…地下得名。山间松林谖造，浓阴匝地，传说老子曾在山…

顶隐居。东峰朝阳峰顶有一平台，登临向上，视野开阔，是观赏日出的著名之处，峰也因此得名。西峰莲花峰是华山最秀丽的山峰，因峰顶有巨石状如莲花而称，神话故事《宝莲灯》中沉香劈山救母即发生于此。玉女峰为中峰，传说春秋时的萧史善吹笙箫，引得秦穆公之女弄玉的爱慕，她毅然抛弃荣华富贵，与萧史隐居此处，人们为这个美丽的爱情故事所感动，因此将这里命名为玉女峰。北峰云台峰顶平如云中之台，三面绝壁，险要异常。1949年，人民解放军智取华山时，一支勇敢的小分队在这里攀登天险，奇袭峰顶，赢得胜利。华山风景区面积达300平方千米，景点众多，各具特色，被列为国家重点风景名胜区。

鸣沙山：又名神沙山，位于甘肃省敦煌市南6千米处，由流沙积成，沙垄相衔，盘亘回环，远望犹如一条横卧的黄色巨龙，山体绵延平滑，山脊陡峭若削，蔚为奇观。鸣沙山东西绵亘40多千米，南北宽20千米，海拔1715米，山体高达几十米。据说人登上沙山，由顶峰下滑，细沙与人体齐泻，伴随鸣声不绝，因此得名。传说古代有位将军率兵出征，几万人马在鸣沙山下宿营。夜晚敌兵来袭，不料，狂风突然大作，顷刻间，全军被黄沙掩埋。从此，山内时闻鼓角之声和战马的嘶鸣声，这更增加了鸣沙山的神秘感。

月牙泉：位于鸣沙山北麓，因一泓碧水在沙丘环抱之中，犹如一弯新月，故名。泉水东深西浅，澄澈见底，有人将它比喻成美丽少女柔情的眼睛。月牙泉水多不溢，干旱不涸。据说，自东汉以来便有此泉记载，两千多年来从未枯竭，创造了沙泉共存的奇迹，被誉为"沙漠第一泉"。泉水中还有不易寻见的铁背鱼和七星草，传说食用后可以长生不老，因此，月牙泉又被称为"药泉"。在这里，蓝天、沙海、碧泉，和谐恬谧，相映成趣，游人无论从山顶鸟瞰，还是在泉边畅游，都会骋怀神往。

雅丹地貌："雅丹"一词源自维吾尔语，原意是指陡峭的土丘。在地质学上，雅丹地貌专指经长期风蚀、由一系列平行的垄脊和沟槽构成的景观。甘肃省敦煌市西北180千米处，有一片雅丹地貌，总面积约400平方千米，其规模之大，形态之奇，实属举世罕见。它的形成经历了大约30万年到70万年的岁月。劲风刮过时，会发出各种怪叫声，犹如千万只野兽在咆哮怒吼，使人毛骨悚然，因而也被人们称为"魔鬼城"。这座特殊的"城"内，集中分布着各种造型奇特、犬牙交错的风蚀地貌，有的状如壁龛、蘑菇、巨柱，有的则如蒙古包、骆驼、雄狮、海龟、佛像等，千姿百态，惟妙惟肖，令人瞠目。这里以它独特的荒漠风光、形态各异的地质景观和古老的民间传说，吸引着无数勇敢的探险者前来探索。

青海湖和鸟岛：青海湖位于青海省东北部，湖面海拔3200米，面积4500多平方千米，是中国最大的内陆湖泊，也是中国最大的咸水湖。青海湖蒙古语称为"库库诺尔"，意为青色的湖。湖周群峰环绕，湖面烟波浩渺，碧波连天，像一块巨大的宝石镶嵌在青藏高原之上。这里气候凉…

即便在烈日炎炎的盛夏，日平均气温一般都在15℃左右，是理想的避暑胜地。位于青海湖西北部的鸟岛被誉为"鸟…的天堂"。鸟岛面积0.8平方千米，每年5月，从东南亚、印度、巴基斯坦以及中国南方各地飞来的斑头雁、天鹅、棕头鸥、鸬鹚、秋沙鸭等多种候鸟，总数在10万只以上…在岛上栖息营巢，蔚为壮观。

日月山：位于青海湖东南，这座在青藏高原算不上大的山…却因为唐朝文成公主远嫁西藏的故事而非常有名。传说…成公主入藏时经过此处，看到山麓两边景色迥异，顿时泪…水连连，思乡之情油然而生。但想起自己肩负的重任，她…毅然将唐太宗赐给的日月宝镜扔下日月山的东坡，以表决…心。此山因宝镜而得名。文成公主在这里流下的泪水，…作了山麓流向独特的倒淌河。这虽说只是一个传说，却反…映了人们对日月山地理位置特殊性的深刻认识。日月山海…拔3500多米，属于祁连山脉的支系，因土色赤红，又名赤…岭。它不仅是青海省农业区和牧业区的自然分界线，还是…中国内流河的内流区和外流区的分界线。山麓西边广袤苍…茫，牛羊遍地；山麓东边却村落点点，麦浪滚滚。想必文…成公主来到这里，看见景色变了，连人们的生活方式也变…了，才真正意识到这座山其实也是她人生的分界线。

沙坡头游览区：位于宁夏回族自治区中卫市西，以大漠黄…河、治沙工程和中国四大鸣沙之一而闻名。北面是著名的…腾格里大沙漠，奔腾的黄河在黑山峡一个急转弯，缓缓流…入中卫境内，造就了沙坡头神奇的自然景观。中国四大鸣…沙之一的金沙鸣钟就在沙坡头的坡顶。游人滑沙，如从天…降，沙坡便发出轰鸣声，沉闷浑厚，犹如金钟长鸣，因此…得名。大河滔滔，沙山陡峭，白云碧空，沙海绿洲，沙坡…头不仅景观独特，还以丰硕的治沙成果饮誉世界，被誉为…"世界沙都"。

Major scenic areas in the West China are as follows:

Qutang Gorge: The Yangtze River, rising from the Qinghai-Tibet Plateau, winds 6,300 kilometers through the country from west to east. When passing through the eastern fringe of Sichuan Basin, the mighty Yangtze River flows violently eastward, like a shape sword cleaving a path through the high and precipitous ridges, thus forming the spectacular world famous Three Gorges: Qutang, Wuxia and Xiling. The Three Gorges of the Yangtze River extend from the western Baidicheng (White Emperor City) in Fengjie County of Chongqing Municipality, to Nanjinguan of Yichang City in Hubei Province in the east, lengthening about 193 kilometers. The abrupt

云南省三江并流景区：梅里雪山…
Meili Snow Mountain of the Three
Parallel Rivers of Yunnan Protected Area

...ills and turbulent current constitute matchless scenery and make it a world-renowned tourist attraction. Of the three gorges, the straight and craggy Qutang Gorge is the shortest and narrowest, yet the most dangerous one. From east to west, it measures 8 kilometers long, and is 150 meters at the widest place while only 50 meters at the narrowest place. With vertical cliffs piercing through the heaven as its two flanks, as well as swash and rumble, the surging Yangtze River pours into the "gateway" with great momentum. Looking up towards the tops of towering steep mountains along the gorge, one sees from a boat only a narrow strip of clouds and sky.

Southern Hot Spring Scenic Area: One of the four most famous springs of Chongqing, the Southern Hot Spring lies in the southern suburbs of the city and 16 kilometers from the city proper. The spring water rises to a temperature of 40 degrees centigrade all year round, and has a good therapeutic effect on many kinds of disease such as rheumatism and dermatosis. As early as the Ming Dynasty (1368-1644) it has been exploited. Thanks to its location at the juncture of Baxian and Tushan mountains and near by the Huaxi (Floral Stream), the scenic area features rolling and wooded ridges, sweet and mild climate, and rich landscape resources including mountain, water, forest, gorge and cave. Dotted in the area are steep peaks, luxuriant forest, springs in various characteristics and mysterious karst caves, and the scenic spots such as Huxiaoquanliu (Stream Hanging at the Huxiaokou), Gongqiaofanyue (Arch Bridge and the Moon) and others are reputed as the Twelve Attractions. Of them, the Huxiaoquanliu is the most famous. The water of Huaxi flows slowly, however when passing through the Huxiaokou (Mouth of Tigers Growling), it suddenly speeds up with mighty torrents and rushes down from the fault, forming a spectacular multi-folded waterfall.

Emei Mountain Scenic Area: The Emei Mountain lies in the southern area of Sichuan basin, 150 kilometers away from Chengdu. It is one of the four Sacred Buddhist Mountains in China, known as the Bodhimanda of Puxian (Samantabhadra Bodhisattva). The whole mountain covers an area of 300 square kilometers, and Wanfoding (Summit of Ten-Thousand Buddhas), the main peak of Emei Mountain, is 3,099 meters in elevation. It features charming scenery, abounds in rainfalls, rare as well as precious animals and plants, which bestow it several monikers:"Buddhist Celestial Mountain", "Kingdom of Plants", "Para-

use of Animals", and "Geological Museum", and is particularly famous for the title, "Elegance of Mt. Emei under the Heaven". The four wonders of Emei Mountain are the Sunrise, Sea of Clouds, Buddha's Halo and the Holy Lamp of Jinding (Golden Summit) which is 3,077 meters high above sea level. Among them, the Sea of Clouds is the most famous. In sunny days, the cloud slowly rises up and in just a few seconds, turns into a vast turbulent sea of clouds. The peaks and ridges, now visible, now hidden assume myriads of shapes like islands in the sea under the dazzling sunlight. What a splendid view! In 1996, the UNESCO inscribed it on the List of World Heritage.

Huanglong Scenic Area: Situated in the Songpan County of the Aba Tibetan and Qiang Ethnic Groups Autonomous Prefecture in Sichuan Province, the Huanglong Scenic Area was named after the ancient Huanglongsi (Yellow Dragon Temple) that built within the area. Covering a total area of 1,340 square kilometers, it consists of such scenic spots as Huanglong Ravine, Danyunxia (Red Rosy Clouds), Hongxingyan (Red Star Rock), Xuebaoding (Snow Precious Summit) and Muni Ravine. Huanglong boasts various huge and exotic landscapes, such as the magnificent mountains, the precipitous valleys, the splendid grassland scenery, the vast sea of forest, plenty of lakes, rich animal-plant resources, and unique folk customs, and these marvelous scenes are quite spectaculars and win the scenic area a reputation of "Holy Land, Paradise and Jade Pond in the World". The Huanglong Ravine is the major scenic spot and provides unique and wild scenery formed by undulating mountains, color lakes, multi-folded waterfalls and magical travertine. Surfaced with sparkling and glittering rocks, the ravine winds its way upwards along mountain slopes resembling a giant yellow dragon and strings colorful lakes and ponds together like a beautiful necklace. All the lakes and ponds are different in shape and depth, and their waters reflect a variety of charming colors. In 1992, it became a world natural heritage site of the UNESCO.

Siguniang Mountain Scenic Area: It is situated at the boundary between Xiaojin and Wenchuan counties of Aba Tibetan and Qiang Ethnic Groups Autonomous Prefecture in Sichuan Province, and comprises four contiguous peaks. According to the local folktale, the mountains were turned into by four beautiful girls, hence the name Siguniang, which means Four Girls Mountain in Chinese. Famous for grandness, straightness and forcefulness, they stand shoulder by

shoulder and are covered by snow all year round amidst clouds. The tallest among four mountains (the fourth one) rises 6,250 meters above sea level, since the Gongga Snow Mountain, the tallest mountain in Sichuan with an elevation of 7,556 meters, is nick-named the "King of Sichuan's Mountains", the Sigunian is known as the "Queen of Sichuan's Mountains". With Minjiang River rushing in the east and Dadu River tearing in the west, the Siguniang Mountain scenic area features temperate climate, abundant rainfall, luxuriant forests and carpet of grasses. Its charming scenery may be compared to that of Southern Europe, so it is also called Oriental Alps Mountain. The scenic area includes Siguniang Mountain, Balang Mountain, Shuangqiao (Double Bridge) Gully, Changping (Long Terrace) Gully and Haizi (Lake) Gully. Among them, Shuangqiao Gully lengthening about 35 kilometers, is extremely attractive. Major scenic spots such as Yangliu (Poplar and Willow) Bridge, Wuse (Five-Hued) Mountain, Lieren (Hunter) Peak, Yinghui (Eagle's Beak) Rock, Jinji (Golden Cock) Ridge and others, all with different postures and colors, presenting a three-dimensional painting gallery.

Qingcheng Mountain: Qingcheng Mountain, southwest to Dujiangyan City proper in Sichuan Province and 66 kilometers from Chengdu City, is one of the birth places of Taoism. Surrounded by countless peaks and densely covered by ancient trees with branches reaching towards the sky all year round, the mountain was named "Qingcheng", meaning Green Town in Chinese. Celebrated for its seclusion, it is formed by conglomerates, and its highest peak is more than 1,600 meters above sea level. The mountain consist of two parts: the anterior and the posterior Qingcheng mountains. The whole scenic area boasts 36 peaks, 8 big caves, 72 lesser caves and 108 scenic spots, as well as 11 Taoism monasteries and temples. The sun rising, sea of clouds and supernatural light are three natural spectacles. It was said that Zhang Daoling, the founder of Taoism, once prayed and even died here, so it was took as one of the Four Most Famous Taoism Mountains, and called the Number Fifth Blessed Spot under Heaven. The Qingcheng Mountain has lavish forests, piles of piles peaks, sheltered winding paths and Taoism monasteries tucked away in the woods.

its principal natural attractions include 1,000-year ginkgo, Jinbian (Golden Whip) Rock, Yuecheng (Moon-City) Lake, Chaoyang (Sun-Facing) Cave, and Natural Painting, etc. In 2000 together with the Dujiang Weir Irrigation System, Qingcheng Mountain was inscribed on the World Heritage List by the UNESCO.

Wolong Nature Reserve: Located in Wenchuan County of Sichuan Province, the Wolong Nature Reserve is lying on the complicated land formations of transition area from the Qinghai-Tibet Plateau to the Sichuan Basin. With luxuriant vegetation and a cool climate, it is a national key nature preservation area designed primarily to protect and reproduce the giant panda, which enjoys the reputation of the "living fossil". In the reserve, peaks shrouded in clouds rise one higher than another, and there are over 4,000 species of plants including such rare plants as Chinese dove tree, larix mastersiana, dipteronia sinensis and cercidiphyllum japonicum, which have a very conspicuous vertical spectrum of vegetation. It differs with different elevations and offers favorable conditions for the preservation of more than 400 kinds of animals and birds, 50-odd of which including giant panda, golden monkey, takin and cervus albirostris are under national protection. All these win Wolong Nature Reserve many monikers: "Hometown to Giant Panda", "Precious Gene Bank of Bios" and "Nature Zoo and Botanical Garden". The reserve also has many scenic spots such as Yingxiong (Hero) Gully and Yinchang (Silver Factory) Gully. The snow-capped mountains, deep gullies, virgin forest, appealing waters, rare flowers and grass, as well as giant pandas strolling leisurely and carefree, golden monkeys frolicking and playing with each other, birds singing sweetly, together constitute a charming scenic resort luring countless tourists and scientists.

Fanjing Mountain: The Fanjing Mountain is located in an area comprising parts of the three counties of Jiangkou, Yinjiang and Songtao in the northeast section of Guizhou Province. It is the major peak of Wuling Mountain, and the highest peak — Fenghuang (Phoenix) Peak is 2,572 meters above sea level. With diversified vegetation and clearly distinguished vertical zones, it is known for its large primeval forests and the only well-preserved primitive forest ecosystem on the same latitude in the world. The area has a dangerous mountain situation, typical karst landform, layer upon layer of peaks, as well as dense forest, and was list as the state-level nature reserve. There are nearly 3,000 kinds of plants in Fanjing Mountain

of which Chinese dove tree, Bretschneidera sinensis, hemlock, Liriodendron chinense and other rare tree varieties are listed as national protected plants, demonstrating the primitive and ancient nature of the components of the tree system in the plant area. Favorable nature conditions also provide an ideal habitation area for wild animals. Over 300 species of birds, amphibious and reptile animals were identified here, of which 17 are national protected animals. In particular, only 100-odd golden monkeys (Rhinopithecus brelichi) are thus far discovered in the world. In 1986, the reserve joined the "Man and Biosphere" nature reserve network of UNESCO.

Huangguoshu Waterfall: Perhaps no scenic spot in Guizhou Province is better known than Huangguoshu Waterfall on Baishui River southwest to Zhenning County of Anshun City. It is China's No.1 waterfall, enjoying the good name of "the marvelous sight in the world". When the water of Baishui River flows to Huangguoshu, the fractured riverbed forces it to form nine-level waterfall with white mist, the largest one being about 81 meters wide. Over-70-meter drop causes an unceasing thunderous sound and shoots a shower of water droplets up to a height of 90 meters, like the Milky Way rushing down with numberless pearls. What a grand and peculiarly attractive scene! A pavilion built on the opposite bank provides a panoramic vista of the spectacle. The waterfall happens to form the curtain for a cave lengthening 134 meters hidden behind it, where makes sense in fairyland and waterfall can be heard, watched and touched.

Yulong Snow Mountain: The Yulong (Jade Dragon) Snow Mountain in Yunnan Province is situated at the northern side of the embankment of Lijiang and 15 kilometers from the city. This magnificent snow-capped mountain sprawls 35 kilometers from north to south and has a width of 20 kilometers from east to west. Looking from afar, the fog-enlaced mountain resembles a jade dragon flying in the clouds, hence the name. It consists of 13 peaks, which all have the altitudes of at least 4,000 meters. Among them, Shanzidou (Fan steep cliff) is the highest one with an altitude of 5,596 meters above sea level, and ranks the second highest in Yunnan Province. The plant resources there are particularly rich. These species live in different temperature levels and create different kinds of views of Jade Dragon Snow Mountain, as well as form an epitome of the plant zone of the Hengduan (Cross-Sectional) Mountain in northwest Yunnan. Hemmed in by snow-mountains and cocooned by

luxuriant vegetation, Yunshanping (Spruce Plateau) is grassland with gigantic spruces. 3,365 meters in elevation, it was a place for young lovers to sacrifice their young lives in honor of true love and to escape from the arranged marriages and feudal ethics in Naxi people's legends.

Lugu Lake: On the border of Ninglang Yi Autonomous County of Yunnan Province and Yanyuan County of Sichuan Province is inlaid a shimmering pearl: Lugu Lake, which occupies an area of almost 52 square kilometers, with an altitude of 2,685 meters and an average depth of 40 meters. The lake is surrounded by high and sublime mountains abounding in forest resources, the water is generally clear and green, and the wooded islands are various in shapes. All these afford an exquisite beauty and charming scenery. However, the Lugu Lake is known around the world not only for its beautiful natural scenery, but also because it is home to a unique matriarchate well-preserved by the indigenous Mosuo people, who are a branch of the Naxi ethnic minority group. They are not united by wedlock, each living at the mother's home respectively, yet keeping a casual cohabitation relationship. It is the living fossil of matriarchal society and is reputed as the "Female's Kingdom in modern times".

Stone Forest Scenic Area: The Stone Forest is in Shilin Yi Ethnic Group Autonomous County, Yunnan Province about 84 kilometers from Kunming, covers a total area of 350 square kilometers and is a typical example of karsts topography. Approximately 270 million years ago, the region was a vast expanse of sea. Later the sea receded due to the movement of the earth's crust and the limestone deposited on the sea bed rose up, and hence formed the land. Over time, weathering and erosion by waters dissolved the stone and finally molded them into groups of pillars, which extend as far as the eye can see, looking like a vast forest of stone, hence the name "the Stone Forest". In scenic area, visitors can enjoy the peculiar sight of the countless stone peaks, as well as huge number of vertically carved, fantastically shaped limestone pillars assuming a thousand different shapes, all lofty and precipitous, charming and enchanting. It is reputed as "the most fantastic scenery under heaven".

Major scenic spots include Big and Small Stone Forests, Naigu Stone Forest, Dadieshui Waterfall, Moon Lake, Subterranean Stone Forest in Zhiyun Cave, and Cave of Magical Wind.

Erhai Lake: Located in Dali City of Yunnan Province, the Erhai Lake is the second largest alpine lake in the province after Dianchi. Implying that the lake is ear-shaped and its waves are as large as a sea's, hence the name, which means "sea shaped like an ear" in Chinese. Covering an area of 250 square kilometers with an average altitude of 1,980 meters above sea level, the lake like a crescent as seen from Cangshan Mountain located on its western bank, and since the ancient time, it has been reputed as a flawless jade inlaid into mountains. In a sunny day, the crystal and rippling waters of Erhai Lake and the snow mantled Cangshan Mountain add radiance and beauty to each other. The scene is, therefore, described as "Silver Mt. Cangshan and Jade Erhai". The most impressive is said to be the Moon of Erhai. When the full moon is mirrored on the lake, Erhai turns to be a unique fairyland: an integral whole moon hanging in the sky sends out bright moonbeams, while the other one echoes on the lake, both enhancing one another's beauty. It is known as one of the four most magnificent sights in Dali, the other three being the Wind of Xiaguan, the Flower of Shangguan and the Snow of Cangshan Mountain.

Dianchi Lake in Kunming: Kunming, an ancient cultural city, is the capital of Yunnan Province. Located in the central part of the province, the city is like spring all the year around, thus enjoying the reputation of being the "Spring City". With its breath-taking scenery, the Dianchi Lake situated at the foot of Xishan (Western Mountain) is one of the most charming attractions of the city. The Dianchi Lake, also called "Kunming Lake" and "Southern Lake of Yunnan" in ancient times, is the largest plateau lake in Yunnan and the sixth largest fresh water lake in China. It is 300 square kilometers in surface area and 1,885 meters in altitude. Besieged by rolling green mountains, it claims to be "a pearl on the Yungui Plateau". The area is dotted with flowers and green plants throughout the year. When the weather is fine, vast expanse of the lake extends to horizon and the limpid water seems to blend with the sky mutually, gentle breeze ripples the lake. Between the cerulean sky and green water are flocculent white clouds as well as flocks of freely flying red-beak gulls, while sailing on the lake are fishing boats

honing and netting. Taking a boat to voyage and breathing the fresh air, what an enjoyable and easy moment it is!

The Himalayas: Being the main body of the Qinghai-Tibet Plateau, Tibet at an average elevation of over 4,000 meters is reputed as the "Roof of the World". Lofty mountains — Tanggula in the north, the Himalayas in the south, Hengduan in the east, Kunlun in the west, and Nyainqentanglha and Gangdise in the center — form the unique topography of Tibet with their astonishing heights. Among them, the Himalayas is located at the southwestern edge of Qinghai-Tibet Plateau. Having an average altitude of more than 6,000 meters and a spanning of 2,400 kilometers, it is the most majestic yet youngest mountain system on the earth, and no other place in the world that possesses such soul-shaking and splendid scenery. Located in Tingri County, the Mt. Qomolangma, is the main peak of the Himalayas and highest peak in the world. Standing 8,844.43 meters above sea level, the peak, snow-capped throughout the year, lies at the border between China and Nepal, and is reputed "the Third Pole" of the earth. Massive glaciers extending 26 kilometers feature a thrilling splendor. The place is actually clustered with 38 peaks at heights of more than 7,000 meters, among which, the Lhotse (8,516 meters), Makalu (8,463 meters), Cho Oyu (8,201 meters) and Shisha Pangma (Gosainthan, 8,012 meters) are all over 8,000 meters above sea level. A vast territory, complex geography and landform, unparalleled scenery of high mountains and plateau, as well as various climates form the endless charms of Himalayas, which lures more and more people from the world traveling, exploring and re-searching seeking.

Huashan Mountain: One of the Five Sacred Mountains in China, Huashan Mountain is located on the eastern part of Guanzhong Plain and south in Huayin City, Shaanxi province, and it was known as the Western Sacred Mountain due to its geographical location in relation to the others. Ever since ancient times, Huashan is noted for being extremely magnificent and precipitous. There is only one perilous passage to the summit. True to its reputation as the "most precipitous mountain under heaven", Huashan boasts a cluster of five peaks: the south Luoyan, the east Chaoyang, the west Lianhua, the central Yunu, and the north Yuntai. The Luoyan (Fallen Wild Goose) Peak rises to 2,200 meters above sea level, making it the highest peak of Huashan. It was said that the wild geese used

to dwell here when they came back from the south hence the name. With perilous cliffs as well as tall and luxuriant pines, the peak presents impressive scenes. Legend has it that Lao Tze once lived here in seclusion. The Chaoyang (Facing the Sun) Peak is a fantastic sight too. On its top there is the "Sun Platform". Towering magnificently over a broad vista of the surroundings, it is a famous place for viewing the sun rise. The Lianhua (Lotus Flower) Peak is the most graceful peak of Huashan. It got its name from a huge rock on its top resembling a lotus flower. It is the place where Chen Xiang rescued his mother by splitting a mountain, a famous fairy tale of ancient China. The Yunu (Jade Maiden) was named after a romantic story. During the Spring and Autumn Period, a young man named Xiao Shi was good at playing bamboo flute. Nong Yu, who was the daughter of the king of the Qin State, fell deeply in love with the young yet poor man and gave up all her riches and honor to marry Xiao. The lovers came here to live for the rest of their life. To commemorate the couple, people gave the peak its present name. As its name implies, the Yuntai (Cloud Platform) Peak has a flat top shrouded in clouds with all its three sides being perilous cliffs. When the main forces of Chiang Kai Shek's was in hasty retreat to Taiwan in 1949, a Kuomintang (KMT) general led his troops up Huashan Mountain, with the idea to fortify his position and wait for the remainder of the KMT forces to arrive. However, a detachment of People's Liberation Army (PLA) climbed up the peak bravely and surprise attacked the enemy which was known as the Ingeniously Taking Huashan Mountain and is one of the PLA's legendary successes in the past. Presently, covering a total area of 300 square kilometers, the Huashan Mountain scenic area is dotted with multitudinous tourist spots with their distinctive characteristics, and is a national scenic resort.

Echoing-Sand Hill: Six kilometers south of the city of Dunhuang, Gansu Province, is the Echoing-Sand Hill which is also known as the Divine-Sand Hill. The hill at an elevation of 1,715 meters is actually made up of smooth-surfaced sand dunes, which, surrounded by rolling ridges and precipitous cliffs, reach a relative height of tens of meters. Stretching over 40 kilometers from east to west with a width of 20 kilometers,

新疆维吾尔自治区火焰山
Flaming Mountain, Xinjiang

The hill offers superb picture-look desert scenery and looks like a gigantic yellow dragon. The sands reportedly make a humming sound when one slides down the sand dunes, hence the name. Legend has it that in ancient time, a general had his tens of thousand soldiers camped in the dunes here. However, enemy attacked them in the dead of night. Suddenly, in the middle of the battle, a fierce wind blew up, filling the sky with sand and burying both armies. Thereafter, the wind blows across the sand's surface to the roll of war drums, as men shouting and horses neighing as well. The legend makes a mystery of the Echoing-Sand Hill.

Crescent Spring: The Crescent Spring is located on the north slopes of Echoing-Sand Hill. It was formed by spring water trickling up into a depression between huge sand dunes, and resembles a crescent, hence the name. The spring is deep in the east and shallow in the west. It is limpid and mirror smooth, so some say it reminds them of the eye of a pretty girl, lucid, beautiful and amorous. You may be wondering how this desert wonder formed. The earliest historical records of the spring date back to the Eastern Han Dynasty (25-220). It has successfully remained unchanged for over two thousand years. And what's more, although given many surprise attacks by sandstorms, it still gurgles clear, and remains worthy as the Number One Spring in the Desert. Legend said the iron-backed fish and seven-starred medicinal herb produced in the lake could prolong life. As a result, the spring is also known as the Medicine Spring. Here, you would feast your eyes on the general view of blue sky, ocean of sands and limpid and blue spring water. No matter where you stand — on the summit of peak or by water — you can't help but marvel at the wondrous sight of the Crescent Spring.

Yadan Wind-Eroded Landform: Yadan, meaning steep small hills in Uygur language, is a wind-eroded landform in arid area. Triassic, Jurassic and cretaceous sedimentary rocks are washed by rainwater and eroded by wind, and, as time goes by, such dazzling landforms are created. The formation process of the yadan landforms took 300,000-700,000 years and ranks first in the world in terms of history and content. About 180 kilometer northwest of Dunhuang is a typical and famous formation of yadan covering an area of over 400 square meters. The largeness of the individual landform of the wholeness and its grotesque configurations are rarely seen in the world. Because of the howling sounds made by the wind, the area is

called the Ghost City by local people. The power of nature produced irregularly shaped ravines, high and low mounds and sculpture-like geologic structures that bear a remarkable resemblance to familiar objects or animals. Inside the "city", some resembling niche, mushroom and gigantic pillar, while others look like Mongolian yurt, camel, lion, turtle, and Buddha statue. There are too much for them to appreciate. The unique scenery and ancient folk tales make it a holy attraction for world's explorers.

Qinghai Lake and Bird Isle: Located in northeast Qinghai Province, 4,500 square kilometers in area and 3,200 meters in elevation, the Qinghai Lake is the largest saltwater lake in China; not only that it is the largest of all lakes, both saltwater and fresh, in the whole country. The Mongolians call it "Koco Nur", which means blue lake. Embraced by rolling mountains, the vast expanse of Qinghai Lake extends to horizon, resembling a huge gem inlaid in the Qinghai-Tibet Plateau. With a pleasant weather, average daily temperature of 15 degrees Celsius in summer, as well as picturesque scenery rimmed by meadowlands and mountains, the Qinghai Lake has all the makings of an ideal summer resort. In the lake Bird Isle is the most charming and attractive place. Situated on the northwestern shore of Qinghai Lake, the isle is a habitat for more than 100,000 migratory birds, including bald-headed geese, geese, brown-headed gulls, cormorants, and ducks, arriving in May from Southeast Asia, India, Pakistan and South China. It is a magnificent sight that so many birds nest and dwell on the island, twitters being carried far and away. The isle is reputed as a "Bird Paradise".

Riyue Mountain: Located southeast to the Qinghai Lake, the Riyue (Sun and Moon) Mountain got very famous because of the Princess Wencheng (?-680) of the Tang Dynasty who married Songtsen Gampo (?-649/650), the king of Tubo, although it couldn't be count as a large mountain in the Qinghai-Tibet Plateau. Legend has it when Princess Wencheng mounted the Riyue Mountain on her way to Tibet and looked wistfully at the land whence she came from and the different scenes on both slopes. She was homesick suddenly and shed tears of sadness. However, she knew how important the task she shouldered, and put the "Precious Sun and Moon Mirror", a gift from the Tang emperor, down the mountain to show her determination. Then her tears turned into the Reverse River on the northwest side of the mountain. This legend perhaps based on the locals' knowledge of the

mountain. The Riyue Mountain, also known as Red Ridge because of its bald reddish rocky top, is more than 3,500 meters in elevation and belongs to the Qilian Mountains. It is not only the natural boundary between the agricultural region and the animal husbandry of Qinghai, but also a line of demarcation between inland rivers and rivers flowing into the sea in China. On the western slopes of the mountain which is covered with luxuriant pasture are herds of cattle and flock of sheep, while on the eastern slopes are scattering villages and sea of wheat. Presumably, when Princess Wencheng came here, she saw the distinguished landscape and life styles, and realized the mountain was also the boundary of her life.

Shapotou Tourist Zone: Shapotou (Top of the Sand Slope) Tourist Area, located in Zhongwei City of Ningxia Hui Autonomous Region, is famous for the Yellow River running through the desert, the desert control project, and the singing sand. It borders the Tenger Desert in north and the Yellow River in south. The galloping Yellow River makes an abrupt turning at Heishan (Black Mountain) Gorge and enters the territory of Zhongwei, bringing up the miraculous natural landscape of Shapotou. One of China's four humming sand dunes, known as "Golden Sand and Humming Bell", is situated at the top of Shapotou. Sliding down the sand dune gives one the ethereal feeling of descending from the sky. The peculiar geological structure of the place causes the sand to emit a bizarre sound like from a resonant golden bell or a large drum, muffled and deep that shocks all around, hence the name. Not only is the Shapotou famous for scenery formed by surging river, steep sand dunes, white clouds, blue sky, ocean of sand and green oasis, but also its success in desertification control program. It was also known as the "Sand Capital in the world".

四川省九寨沟风光
Beautiful Sight of Jiuzhaigou
Scenic Area, Sichuan Province

九寨沟风景名胜区
Jiuzhaigou Scenic Area

九寨沟风景名胜区位于四川省阿坝藏族羌族自治州九寨沟县境内，因沟内坐落的9座藏族村寨而得名。风景区总面积1320平方千米，自然风光优美，集翠海、叠瀑、森林、雪山、藏族文化风情于一体，有"童话世界"、"人间仙境"的美誉。

"黄山归来不看岳，九寨归来不看水"，九寨沟的水自然天成，清洁纯净，色彩丰富，闻名中外。景区内散布有114个翠海，传说，很久很久以前，一位叫做达戈的男神爱上了美丽的女神沃洛色嫫。他用风云精心磨制了一面宝镜送给心上人。不料魔鬼前来干扰，女神不慎失手打破了宝镜，碎片跌落到人间，变成了九寨沟这114个晶莹的翠海。此外，九寨沟还有47眼泉水、17组瀑布群、11段激流和5处钙华滩流，主要集中在岷山山脉中呈"丫"字形分布的树正、日则和则查洼三条主沟之内，总长度约55千米。九寨沟的水，数量虽众，却千颜万色，多彩多姿，各具特色，幻化无穷。其中，树正群海是九寨沟秀丽风景的大门，全长13.8千米，共有各种湖泊40余个，约占景区全部湖泊的40%，水光潋滟，碧波荡漾，鸟鸣雀唱，堪称一路美景。

九寨沟四季景色都十分迷人。春季，冰消雪化，瀑流泉涌，蜂飞蝶舞，百花争妍，团团簇簇吐芳菲；夏季，微风凉爽，苍翠欲滴，银屑般的瀑布恣意抒发着激情；秋季，五彩斑斓的秋叶倒映在澄澈明丽的水中，与湖面缤纷的落英相映成趣；冬天，这里则成了一个晶莹别透的冰雪世界，诗情画意，宁静悠远。九寨沟童话世界般的四季，极富神韵和魅力，展示着自然造化中最美丽的景致。景区内动植物种类十分丰富，原始森林遍布，还栖息着大熊猫、金丝猴、天鹅等珍贵野生动物。

九寨沟风景区内著名的景点有宝镜岩、盆景滩、芦苇海、火花海、卧龙海、树正瀑布、犀牛海、诺日朗瀑布、镜海、珍珠滩瀑布、五花海、熊猫海、剑竹海、天鹅海、芳草海、悬泉、剑岩、长海、五彩池、上下季节海等。

九寨沟是中国著名的世界级景区，拥有世界自然遗产、世界人与生物圈保护区、绿色环球21、国家AAAA级景区等多项桂冠。

Located in the Aba Tibetan and Qiang Ethnic Groups Autonomous Prefecture in Sichuan Province, Jiuzhaigou (literally, Nine-Village Gully) got its name from nine Tibetan villages scattered throughout the valley. An integration of unrivalled emerald lakes, multi-layered waterfalls, lush forests and snowcapped mountains with Tibetan culture and customs, the scenic area with an area of 1,320 square kilometers is reputed as the "Fairyland" and "Wonderland on the earth".

There is a saying that "you have no wish to visit any of Five Sacred Mountains after viewing the Huangshan Mountain and you do not even wish to visit any water after you come back from a trip to Jiuzhaigou." It is truly so. The water of Jiuzhaigou is widely known for its crystal clearness, pure transparency and rich colors. Scattering in the area are 114 sparkling emerald lakes. A long, long time ago, so the legend goes, a male god named Dage fell in love with the beautiful goddess Woluo Semo. One day, he gifted her with an elaborate-designed precious mirror made out of wind and clouds. However, because of interference of an unexpected evil, the goddess happened to break the mirror. Its broken pieces scattered across the world of mortals and turned into 114 gem-like lakes inlaid among mountains forests in the area. In the shape of a capital character "Y", the Jiuzhaigou Scenic Area comprises of three gullies: Shuzheng, Rize and Zezhawa respectively, lengthening about 55 kilometers in total. Besides 114 lakes, there are also 47 springs, 17 waterfalls, 11 torrents and 5 calcifications of various sizes and characteristics, all blending in harmony with each other. The scenic spot of Shuzhengqunhai (Shuzheng Lakes) is the entrance to magnificent Jiuzhaigou. With a total length of 13.8 kilometers, it contains more than 40 different lakes, occupying 40 per cent of the total area in Jiuzhaigou. The water is bright blue and crystal lucid, ripples spread easily, and the birds sing ditties, forming a living colorful gallery.

Jiuzhaigou has a pleasant weather, and its charming scenery changing during different seasons attracts tourists all the year round. When spring is coming, the ice and snow begin to melt and spring water begins to rise. All the flowers contend in beauty and fascination, and the air is filled with the fragrance of blossoms, luring many dancing bees and butterflies. It is cool and pleasant in the summer, the breeze is gentle, and silver waterfalls fly down deeply seemed to be filled with enthusiasm. Jiuzhaigou becomes drenched with verdant green, while the scenery is very appealing and enchanting. In golden autumn, the leaves turn crimson on the trees. Bright-colored autumn leaves mirror on the translucent lakes setting off with the fallen petals float in the water. In winter, mountains and woods are coated in snow, and the gully becomes especially quiet presenting a picturesque scene of ice and snow world. Jiuzhaigou, a fairy land gifted by nature, is full of charms with its seasonal scenery. And what's more, Jiuzhaigou, a natural botanical and zoological garden, is a home to densely growing conifers and broadleaf trees, and of rare and endangered animal species such as the giant panda, golden monkey, and swan.

Major scenic spots in Jiuzhaigou are Precious Mirror Cliff, Potted Landscape Shoal, Reed Lake, Sparking Lake, Sleeping Dragon Lake, Shuzheng Waterfall, Rhinoceros Lake, Nuorilang Waterfall, Mirror Lake, Pearl-Shoal Waterfall, Five Flowers Lake, Giant Panda Lake, Sword Bamboo Lake, Swan Lake, Fragrant Grass Lake, Hanging Spring, Sword Cliff, Long Lake, Five-Hued Pond, Upper Season Lake, Lower Season Lake, and so on.

Jiuzhaigou, as the sole scenic spot, has gained a good few of laurels including world natural heritage site, participant of Green Global 21, Global Man and the Biosphere Programme and 4-A Scenic Area at the state level, making it world-famous.

四川省九寨沟树正瀑布
Shuzheng Waterfalls of Jiuzhaigou
Scenic Area, Sichuan Province

1—3 四川省九寨沟风光
Beautiful Sight of Jiuzhaigou
Scenic Area, Sichuan Province

四川省黄龙风景名胜区
Huanglong Scenic Area,
Sichuan Province

1.四川省峨眉山仙境
**Wonderland of Emei Mountain,
Sichuan Province**

2.四川省峨眉山风景区
**Emei Mountain Scenic Area,
Sichuan Province**

3.四川省峨眉山金刚岩
**Jingangyan (Diamond Rock) of the
Emei Mountain, Sichuan Province**

四川省蜀南竹海
Bamboo Sea in South of
Sichuan Province

四川省丹巴县大渡河激流
Surging Waves of Dadu River,
Danba County, Sichuan Province

1.四川省米亚罗风景区秋色
Miyaluo Scenic Resort in
Autumn, Sichuan Province

2.3.四川省稻城县仙乃日雪山
Xiannairi Snow Mountain,
Daocheng County, Sichuan Province

四川省亚丁保护区红草地
Red Grassland in Yading Protected Area,
Sichuan Province

四川省海螺沟雪山雄姿
Imposing Snow Mountains in Hailuogou
(Conch Gully), Sichuan Province

1. 四川省海螺沟连绵雪峰
Rolling Snow Mountains in Hailuogou Scenic Area, Sichuan Province

2. 四川省海螺沟日照金山
Golden Mountain in Sunshine, Hailuogou Scenic Area, Sichuan Province

3. 四川省海螺沟冰川及冰舌
Glaciers and Ice Tongue, Hailuogou Scenic Area, Sichuan Province

四川省四姑娘山风景区
Siguniang Mountain Scenic Area,
Sichuan Province

3

1-4 四川省卧龙自然保护区中的国家重点保护动物：
(1)大熊猫；(2) 金丝猴；(3) 白唇鹿；(4) 白臀鹿．
Animals under national protection in the Wolong Nature Reserve: (1) Giant Panda; (2) Golden Monkey; (3) Cervus albirostris; (4) Cervus elaphus.

5.重庆市地缝奇观
Nature Wonder of "Giant Crack on the Earth", Chongqing Municipality

6.重庆市长江瞿塘峡
Qutang Gorge of the Yangtze River, Chongqing Municipality

7.重庆市南温泉风景区
Southern Hot Spring Scenic Area, Chongqing Municipality

重庆市长江瞿塘峡
Qutang Gorge of the Yangtze River,
Chongqing Municipality

贵州省黄果树瀑布
Huangguoshu Waterfall,
Guizhou Province

贵州省黄果树瀑布
Huangguoshu Waterfall,
Guizhou Province

贵州省梵净山风景区
Fanjing Mountain Scenic Resort,
Guizhou Province

贵州省梵净山风景区
Fanjing Mountain Scenic Resort,
Guizhou Province

三江并流
Three Parallel Rivers of Yunnan Protected Areas

三江并流自然景观位于云南省西北部地区。"三江并流"是指源自青藏高原的金沙江、澜沧江和怒江三条大河流入横断山脉纵谷地带后，并行奔流的壮观景象。其中，澜沧江与金沙江的最短直线距离为66千米；澜沧江与怒江的最短距离仅19千米。整个区域包括了丽江地区、迪庆藏族自治州和怒江傈僳族自治州境内的9个自然保护区和10个风景名胜区，总面积达1.7万多平方千米，划分为高黎贡山、白茫—梅里雪山、哈巴雪山、千湖山、红山、云岭、老君山和老窝山八大片区。2003年7月，联合国教科文组织世界遗产委员会将这一罕见的自然景观列入《世界遗产名录》。

三江并流景区堪称是一部地球演化历史的教科书。四五千万年前，印度板块与欧亚大陆板块发生碰撞，古特提斯海不断退缩，引发喜马拉雅山和青藏高原的隆起，从而促成了横断山脉的形成，并造就了三江并行奔流这一世界独有的自然奇观。由于处在东亚、南亚和青藏高原三大地理区域的交汇处，它成为世界上罕见的高山地貌及其演化的代表地区。

三江并流是世界生物多样性最丰富的地区之一，被誉为"世界生物基因库"。由于该地区没有受第四纪冰期大陆冰川的覆盖，并且区域内遍布南北走向的山脉，为欧亚大陆生物南来北往提供了通道和避难所，因而成为欧亚大陆生物群落最富集的地区。这里汇集了全国20%以上的高等植物和全国25%的动物种数，其中包括秃杉、桫椤、红豆杉等国家级保护植物，以及滇金丝猴、羚羊、雪豹、孟加拉虎、黑颈鹤等国家重点保护动物。

除了拥有三江并流奇观之外，这一地区还汇集了高山、峡谷、冰川、雪峰、高原、湿地、森林、草甸、湖泊等不同类型的地貌景观，各类景点难计其数，可以说是北半球除沙漠和海洋景观外各类自然景观的缩影，主要包括：梅里雪山、老窝山、老君山、红山、千湖山、哈巴雪山、高黎贡山、白茫雪山、云岭、小黑山、大雪山、碧塔海、怒江大峡谷、纳帕海、白水台、虎跳峡、长江第一弯等。

碧塔海：位于香格里拉县城东北25千米处的深山密林间，海拔约3539米。湖面长3000米，宽不足1000米，湖水平均水深20米，为断层构造湖。碧塔海群山环抱，水清如镜，恬静安谧。四周山岭上有浓绿高大的苍松古栎和枝叶繁茂的杜鹃。花开时节，群芳吐艳，千姿百态，碧塔海犹如戴上一个美丽的花环，香飘数里，景致迷人。残败的杜鹃花飘落湖中，湖中游鱼争相来食。由于杜鹃花略有毒性，游鱼食后便如醉汉一般昏迷不醒，鱼肚朝天漂浮在水面上，形成了碧塔海一大生态奇观——"杜鹃醉鱼"。

香格里拉："香格里拉"，英语为世外桃源之意。此词最早出现在英国作家希尔顿所著《消失的地平线》一书，指书中所描述的和平、宁静的地方。三江并流地区是一处拥有雪山、峡谷、森林、草甸、河流和湖泊的人间秘境，尤其是迪庆藏族自治州充满诗意和梦幻般的田园风光，与书中的描述极为相似。在这片与世隔绝的天地中，永远只有翠绿的青山、在云中出没的民舍、成片的农田、灿烂的阳光、清新的空气和悠闲恬静的生活，令人心驰神往。2001年12月，迪庆自治州的中甸县正式更名为香格里拉。

梅里雪山：位于德钦县东北，是云南最壮观的雪山群，绵延百里，横亘天际，云蒸霞蔚，幻影迭出，被誉为"世界上最美的山"。由于这一地区垂直气候明显，气候变化无常，强烈的上升气流和南下的大陆冷空气相遇，使群山终年积雪覆盖，云遮雾罩，显得缥缈神秘。仅海拔6000米以上的雪峰就有10多座，统称作"太子十三峰"。耸立于群峰之上的卡格博峰，是梅里雪山的主峰，藏语意为"雪山之神"，海拔6740米，为云南第一峰，是藏传佛教中的神山。虽然人类已征服了世界最高的珠穆朗玛峰，但由于卡格博峰复杂的地形和变化莫测的气候，至今仍无人成功登顶。

白水台：位于香格里拉县东南三坝乡境内，距县城100千米，海拔2380米。由于含碳酸钙较高的泉水从山顶流下，经阳光照射发生分解反应，天长日久便形成了白色碳酸钙泉华。从远处望去，白水台犹如用一块巨大的汉白玉雕刻而成，又似一道凝固的瀑布悬于林间，蔚为奇观；在近处观看，则因其形如层层梯田，又被称为"仙人遗田"。白水台不仅风光优美，还是纳西族文化发祥地之一。据说，纳西族东巴教的第一始祖从西藏学习佛经回来，路过白水台，被其美景吸引，因此留下来传教。

虎跳峡：位于玉龙雪山和哈巴雪山之间，距香格里拉县约105千米，是世界上最著名的大峡谷之一。金沙江奔流至此，突被两岸山峦夹峙收成一束，形成这一惊险奇绝的自然景观。虎跳峡全长17千米，分为上虎跳、中虎跳和下虎跳三段，江面最宽处约50米，最窄处仅30米，落差达213米，共18处险滩。其中，上虎跳位于金沙江入口处，为最窄的一段，峡谷两侧险峰耸天，激流从此通过，白浪翻滚，惊涛怒吼，震人魂魄，煞是壮观。江心有一块巨石，相传猛虎曾借此石跃过大江，虎跳峡也因此而得名。

怒江大峡谷：怒江，奔腾于高黎贡山和怒山之间，发源于青藏高原的唐古拉山，全长2800多千米，在我国境内长1540千米，向南奔腾急流，进入缅甸后，称萨尔温江。怒江两岸的山岭多在3000米以上，因落差大，水浪极高，十分壮观。怒江峡谷是世界著名的大峡谷之一，长约300余千米，平均深度约2000米，享有"神秘的东方大峡谷"之誉。江东与西藏交界处的牙关河有两处落差达800米和400米的瀑布，为怒江大峡谷中最壮观的地段。

Located in the mountainous northwest of Yunnan Province, the Three Parallel Rivers site features sections of the upper reaches of three great rivers of Asia: the Yangtze, Mekong and Salween, namely the Jinsha, Lancang and Nujiang rivers, all originated from the Qinghai-Tibet Plateau, run roughly parallel through steep gorges of the Hengduan Mountains. The straight distance between the Lancang and Jinsha rivers is 66 kilometers while that between the Lancang and Nujiang rivers is no more than 19 kilometers. It covers a total of 1.7 million hectares, comprising 9 nature reserves and 10 scenic resorts in Lijiang Area, Diqing Tibetan Autonomous Prefecture and Nujiang Lisu Autonomous Prefectures. The whole area includes 8 geographical clusters, and they are Gaoligong Mountain, Baimang-Meili Snow Mountain, Haba Snow Mountain, Qianhu Mountain, Hongshan Mountain, Yunling Mountain, Laojun Mountain and Laowo Mountain respectively. In July 2003, the site was inscribed on the World Heritage List as a natural property at the 27th session of the UNESCO's World Heritage Committee.

The Three Parallel Rivers site is a veritable museum displaying the geological history of the last

40-50 million years associated with the collision of the Indian Plate with the Eurasian Plate, the closure of the ancient Tethys Sea and the uplifting of the Himalaya Range and Tibetan Plateau, which gave birth to the Hengduan Mountains as well as the unique and marvelous natural phenomenon of three parallel rivers. In addition, the site is located where the three geological regions of East Asia, South Asia and Qinghai-Tibet Plateau, making it a representative of rare alpine landforms and their evolution in the world.

The site of Three Parallel Rivers is reputed to be the "Biological Gene Bank of the World". Because it was not covered by the Quaternary glaciers and most mountains lie from north to south, the area functions as a corridor and sanctuary for biological species of the Eurasian Continent, making it one of the richest biodiversity areas in the world. Today, the region is home to more than 20 per cent of higher plants and 25 per cent of animal species of China, including Taiwania cryptomerioides, Cyathea Spinulosa, Taxaceae and other species of rare plants under state-class protection, while such state-level protected animals as Rhinopithecus bieti, antelope, snow leopard, Bengali tiger and black-necked crane and others.

The area boasts not only spectacle of three parallel rivers, but also every kind of landscape to be found in the northern Hemisphere other than desert and ocean including snow-capped mountains, glaciers, valleys, alpine wetlands, forests, meadows, freshwater lakes, and so on. Among its countless scenic spots, the principle ones are Meili Snow Mountain, Laowo Mountain, Laojun Mountain, Hongshan Mountain, Gaoligong Mountain, Baimang Snow Mountain, Haba Snow Mountain, Qianhu Mountain, Yunling Mountain, Lesser Heishan Mountain, Great Snow Mountain, Bitahai, Nujiang Great Valley, Baishuitai, Hutiaoxia and the Number One Turn of the Yangtze River.

Bitahai Lake of the Three Parallel Rivers of Yunnan Protected Areas: Situated among the dense for-ests in the deep mountains of 25 kilometers northeast of Shangri-La County, the lake has an elevation of 3,539 meters. This fault structural lake is 3,000 meters long and no more than 1,000 meters wide with an average depth of 20 meters, and remains emerald all year round. Surrounded by mountains covered with dense forests of pines and oaks as well as azaleas, the lake resembles a *beryl* inlaid among them. In May every year, azaleas are in full blossom in various shapes, like a big wreath. The hillsides seem to be dyed with different colors and thick perfume makes visitors intoxicated. When the wind blows the petals into the lake, all of the fish vie with each other to eat them. Due to the azalea possessing a little toxicity, the fish are in comas after they eat the petals, then they seem drunk and float on the water surface belly-up, forming an enchanting sight known as the "Fish Drunk on Azaleas' Petals".

Shangri-La *of the Three Parallel Rivers of Yunnan Protected Areas*: "Shangri-La" means a fictitious land of peace in English. The word first appeared in a novel entitled *Lost Horizon* by British novelist James Hilton (1900-1954). The actor in novel happened to reach a place where has snow-capped mountains, gorges forests, grasslands and lakes, and the beautiful scenery made people linger. The peaceful and tranquil place is something alike to the Three Parallel Rivers of Yunnan Protected Areas, especially Diqing Tibetan Autonomous Prefecture. On the land secluded from the world are only mountains covered with luxuriant trees, houses hidden in clouds, seas of fields, bright sunlight and fresh air. It is an idyllic and picturesque fairyland in the world. In December 2001, name of Zhongdian County in Diqing was officially changed into Shangri-La.

Meili Snow Mountain of the Three Parallel Rivers of Yunnan Protected Areas: The Meili Snow Mountain in the northeast of Deqin County is the most magnificent mountain in Yunnan Province. With the snow-capped peaks extending to the horizon, it is extolled as the "most beautiful mountain in the world". In this area, strong updrafts meet with continental cold air masses, forming thick fog and heavy snow. Peaks wreathed in clouds are permanently covered with snow, creating a mysterious and charming scene here. Over 10 peaks are more than 6,000 meters above sea level and are collectively known as the Thirteen Peaks of Prince. Standing imposingly amongst them, the Kagebo Peak with an elevation of 6,740 is the main peak of Meili. It is the tallest in Yunnan, and the Holy Mountain in Lamaism. Despite the fact that man has long since conquered Mt. Qomolangma, the Kagebo, protected by perpendicular cliffs and a treacherous climate, is still a virgin peak, and no one has so far ascended the peak.

Baishuitai of the Three Parallel Rivers of Yunnan Protected Areas: The Baishuitai (White-Water Terrace) is located in Sanba Township, about 100 kilometers southeast to Shangri-La County. With an elevation of 2,380 meters, it is a spectacular karst terrain formed by sediment of calcium carbonate. The top of the terrace features a semicircular platform pool, and spring water rising from the mountaintop flows downward. Over many eons, calcium carbonate crystals contained in the stream water have accumulated wherever the stream flows, forming the impressive sinter. Visitors can see from a faraway place that it like being made of a gigantic white marble, or resembles a solid waterfall hanging among the forest, while from a near place it looks like the terraced fields, so the local people also called it the "Paddy Fields created by the Fairies". The Baishuitai is also the cradle of Dongba Culture of the Naxi People. It is said that, on his way back from Tibet, the founding father of Dongba Culture was attracted by the beautiful scenery here and settled to spread his beliefs.

Hutiaoxia of the Three Parallel Rivers of Yunnan

Protected Areas: About 105 kilometers southeast of Shangri-La County, the Hutiaoxia (Tiger Leaping Gorge) lying between Yulong and Haba snow mountains, is one of the most renowned gorges in the world. When the fast flowing Jinsha River reaches here, the river water is squeezed by mountains on both banks into a narrow gorge, form the marvelous spectacle. The gorge is 17 kilometers in length with a drop of 213 meters and 18 dangerous shoals. The widest surface of the river is 50 meters and the narrowest is only 30 meters. The gorge is naturally divided into three sections: Upper, Middle and Lower, of which the Upper Tiger Leaping Gorge is the mouth of the Jinsha River and the narrowest section. Perilous mountains on both sides tower into the sky and torrents of the water are rolling down. It is alarmingly dangerous and magnificent, and mountains echo with the deafening sound of the roaring water, which could be heard several kilometers away. Here in the midst of the river is a large rock. An ancient legend says that a tiger used this rock as its stepping stone so it could leap across from one side of the gorge to the other, which is how the gorge got its name.

Nujiang River Grand Canyon of the Three Parallel Rivers of Yunnan Protected Areas: The Nujiang River originates from the Tangula Mountain on Qinghai-Tibet Plateau, cuts through the Hengduan Mountains on its way down south and rolls down between the Gaoligong and Nushan mountains. With a total length of more than 2,800 kilometers, the river is 1,540 kilometers in China, and when flowing torrentially into Burma, it was known as the Salween River. Most of mountains along its banks rise to 3,000 meters high, and the falling head and the extremely high waves are very magnificent. The Nujiang River Grand Canyon having a length over 300 kilometers and an average depth of about 2,000 meters, is one of the most famous canyons in the world and reputed as the "mysterious canyon of the Orient". To the east of the river are two waterfalls with a falling head of 800 meters and 400 meters respectively with Yaguan (Mandibular Joint) River on the border of Tibet. It is the most magnificent section of the Nujiang Grand Canyon.

云南省三江并流景区，碧塔海
Bitahai Lake of the Three Parallel Rivers of Yunnan Protected Areas

云南省三江并流景区：碧塔海
Bitahai Lake of the Three Parallel Rivers of Yunnan Protected Areas

云南省三江并流景区：香格里拉
Shangri-la of the Three Parallel Rivers of Yunnan Protected Areas

Meili Snow Mountain of the Three
Parallel Rivers of Yunnan Protected Areas

云南省三江并流景区：梅里雪山
Meili Snow Mountain of the Three
Parallel Rivers of Yunnan Protected Areas

云南省三江并流景区：白茫雪山
Baimang Snow Mountain of the Three
Parallel Rivers of Yunnan Protected Areas

1

1.云南省三江并流景区：虎跳峡
   Hutiaoxia of the Three Parallel Rivers
   of Yunnan Protected Areas

2.云南省三江并流景区：白水台
   Baishuitai of the Three Parallel Rivers
   of Yunnan Protected Areas

3.云南省三江并流景区：怒江大峡谷
   Nujiang River Grand Canyon of the
   Three Parallel Rivers of Yunnan Protected Areas

4.云南省三江并流景区：金沙江大峡谷
   Jinsha River Grand Canyon of the Three
   Parallel Rivers of Yunnan Protected Areas

2

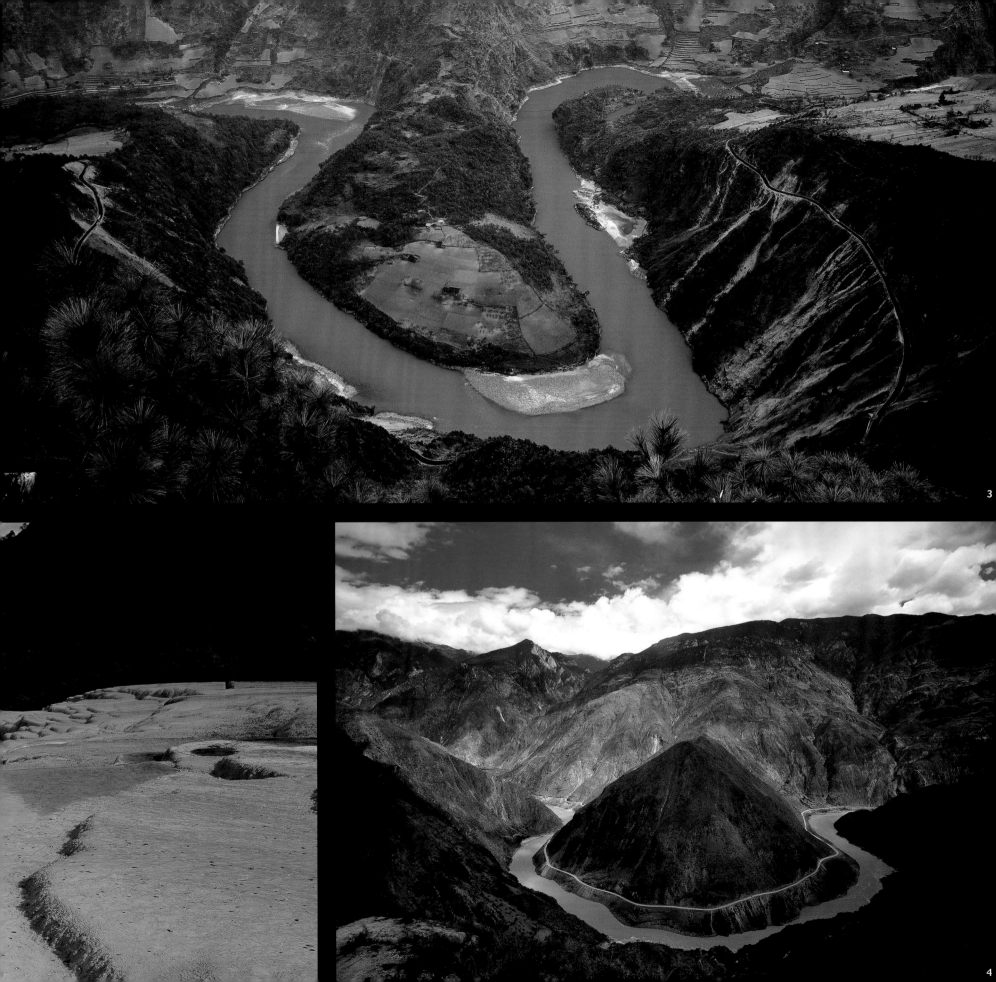

云南省三江并流景区：长江第一弯
Number One Turn of the Yangtze River of
the Three Parallel Rivers of Yunnan Protected Areas

1. 云南省三江并流景区：澜沧江大峡谷
Lancang River Grand Canyon of the Three Parallel Rivers of Yunnan Protected Areas

2. 云南省丽江市玉龙雪山
Yulong Snow Mountain, Lijiang City, Yunnan Province

云南省石林风景区
Stone Forest Scenic Area,
Yunnan Province

云南省石林风景区
Stone Forest Scenic
Area, Yunnan Province

1.云南省楚雄彝族自治州土林风景区
Earth Forest Scenic Area of Chuxiong Yi
Ethnic Group Autonomous Prefecture,
Yunnan Province

2.3.云南省红河哈尼族彝族自治州元阳梯田
Terraced Fields of Yuanyang County,
Honghe Hani and Yi Ethnic Groups
Autonomous Prefecture, Yunnan Province

云南省大理市洱海风景区
Erhai Lake in Dali City,
Yunnan Province

云南省泸沽湖风景区
Lugu Lake Scenic Area
of Yunnan Province

西藏的河湖
Rivers and lakes in Tibet

西藏一直被描述成降水稀少、苍茫辽阔的景象，水乡似乎成为了江南的专利，但事实是：西藏是我国水资源最为丰富的地区。在雪域高原的众山之中，遍布江河湖泊和巨大的冰川。据统计，西藏境内流域面积大于1万平方千米的河流有20多条，流域面积大于2000平方千米的河流有100条以上，许多亚洲著名河流的上源都在这里。此外，西藏还有星罗棋布的大小湖泊1500多个，其中面积超过1000平方千米的有纳木错、色林错和扎西南木错，面积超过100平方千米的湖泊有47个。湖泊总面积24183平方千米，约占全国湖泊总面积的三分之一。著名河湖如下：

雅鲁藏布江：为西藏第一大河，被藏族视为"摇篮"和"母亲河"。雅鲁藏布江发源于喜马拉雅山北麓的杰马央宗冰川，由西向东横贯西藏南部，在中国境内全长2057千米，是世界上海拔最高的大河。雅鲁藏布江主要有五大支流——拉萨河、帕隆藏布、多雄藏布、尼洋曲和年楚河。河水流入印度后被称为布拉马普特拉河。河水流至米林县折向东北，围绕喜马拉雅山东段尾闾的最高峰——南迦巴瓦峰作一马蹄形大拐弯，形成了世界上最深、最长的峡谷，谷深达5300余米，非常壮观。

拉萨河：发源于海拔5020米的米拉雪山，是雅鲁藏布江的五大支流之一。河水流经墨竹工卡县、达孜县，在拉萨市南郊汇入雅鲁藏布江，干流全长551千米，流域面积近3万平方千米。拉萨河两岸山峰多在3600米以上，拥有丰富的高原动植物及地热资源。1300多年前，吐蕃赞普松赞干布迁都拉萨，修宫、建寺，使这里逐渐成为西藏的政治、经济、宗教、文化的中心区域，因此拉萨河又被誉为拉萨市的母亲河。

纳木错：位于当雄县境内，藏语意为"天湖"，面积1961平方千米，湖面海拔4718米，是世界最高的咸水湖，为西藏四大圣湖之一。湖中，五个岛屿兀立于万顷碧波之中，岛上怪石嶙峋，峰林遍布，佛教徒认为其为五方佛的化身，凡去圣湖朝佛敬香者，无不虔诚顶礼膜拜。海拔7162米的念青唐古拉山坐落在湖畔。湖面平静如镜，湖水湛蓝，山峰白雪皑皑，相映成趣，蔚然壮观。纳木错生态资源丰富，湖中盛产多种鱼类，湖区还生产虫草、贝母、雪莲等名贵药材。湖滨平原牧草良好，是天然的牧场，湖泊周围还常有野牦牛、野驴、狐狸等野生动物栖居。

然乌湖：位于昌都地区八宿县境内，面积22平方千米，湖面海拔高度3850米，是藏东南地区最大的湖泊。湖水源于拉古冰川的融雪，是雅鲁藏布江的主要支流帕隆藏布江的源头。湖面狭长，湖水碧蓝清澈，湖畔碧草如茵，与皑皑的雪峰一起组成了如诗如画的景色。

羊卓雍错：位于山南地区浪卡子县和贡嘎县之间，藏语意为"碧玉草原之湖"。海拔4441米，面积600多平方千米，与纳木错、玛旁雍错、拉姆拉错一起被誉为"西藏四大圣湖"。羊卓雍错是西藏湖泊中形状最不规则的湖泊，南宽北窄，岸线曲折，湖区水草丰美，是以放牧半细毛羊为主的牧区。

错高湖：位于林芝地区工布江达县的原始森林中，藏语中意为"绿色的水"，是红教的著名神湖。错高湖状如新月，虽然面积仅36平方千米，却妩媚多姿，有"静卧在绿色绒毯上的仙女"的妙喻。秋天是错高湖最美的时候，湖边是层层叠叠的金色和火红的秋叶，湖水清澈见底，与四周的雪山相应成辉，色彩极为丰富。

班公错：位于阿里地区北部日土县，面积604平方千米，东西长约155千米，南北宽15千米，最窄处仅40米，是我国最长的湖泊。班公错属高原内陆湖泊，湖水补给主要依赖四周山地的冰雪融化。奇特的是，东段湖水是淡水，西段则是咸水。湖上分布几个大大小小的岛屿，其中最著名的为鸟岛。鸟岛面积不大，长约300米，宽200多米，每年却吸引数以万计鸟类在此生息繁衍，主要有斑头雁、棕头鸥、黑颈鹤、蓝点颏等。

Speaking of Tibet, we can't help reminding of the boundless land, few rainfalls, and seemly the title of "land of lakes and rivers" refers in particular to the regions south of the Yangtze River. The opposite is the case. Tibet's water resources rank top in China. The Land of Snow is crisscrossed by rivers. At least 20 of them have a drainage area of more than 10,000 square kilometers; and more than 100 of them claims a valley of more than 2,000 square kilometers. Many mighty rivers of Asia have their upper reaches on the land. Additionally, ensconced in tall mountains and scattered on the vast land are over 1,500 lakes, with a total area of 24,183 square kilometers, or one third of the total acreage of lakes in China. Among them, the Namco Lake, Siling Co and Zhari Namco are larger than 1,000 square kilometers, and 47 other lakes are larger than 100 square kilometers. Some of famous rivers and lakes in Tibet are as follows:

Yarlung Zangbo: The mightiest river of Tibet, Yarlung Zangbo, 2,057-kilometer-long in China, is regarded by Tibetans as the mother river that has nurtured their civilization. Having its origin in the Jiemayangzong Glacier in the northern slopes of the Himalayas, the river runs ferociously from west to east in the south of Tibet, and is widened by numerous tributaries, of which the five largest are the Lhasa River, Parlung Zangbo, Doxung Zangbo, Nyang Qu and Nyainchu respectively. It is the highest river on the earth, and when flowing in India, the river is called the Brahmaputra. On the border between Mainling and Medog counties in east Tibet, the river plunges head-on into Namjagbarwa Mountain in the eastern section of Himalayas, and, making a dramatic turn, turns itself into a formidable canyon in the shape of a colossal horseshoe. With a depth of more than 5,300 meters, it is the deepest and longest canyon in the world.

Lhasa River: One of the five main tributaries of Yarlung Zangbo, the Lhasa River rises in the 5,020-meter-high Mila Snow Mountain. Flowing across Maizhokunggar and Dagze counties, it empties into the Yarlung Zangbo in the southern suburbs of Lhasa City, totally lengthening about 551 kilometers. The river boasts abundant flora and fauna and subterranean heat resource, and takes high peaks being 3,600 meters above sea level as its flanks. With a drainage area of nearly 30,000 square kilometers, it has been reputed as the "Mother River of Lhasa City". That base on the truth that as early as 1,300 years ago, Songtsen Gampo, King of Tobo, moved his capital and had palace and monasteries built there, henceforth, the area became Tibet's political, economic, religious and cultural center gradually.

Namco Lake: Namco, meaning the Heavenly Lake in Tibetan, is located near Damxung. 4,718 meters above sea level and covering a total of 1,961 square kilometers, the lake is the highest saltwater lake in the world, and respected as one of the Four Holy Lakes in Tibet by Buddhist pilgrims. Five islets, planting themselves in the vast sapphire blue lake, is said to be the incarnation of the Buddha of Five Directions. Every pilgrim circumambulating the lake will piously worship them. The snow capped Mt. Nyainqen Tanglha, 7,162 meters in altitude, soars up to sky beside the lake, forming a delightful contrast. Singing streams converge into the clean sapphire blue lake, which looks like a huge mirror framed and dotted with flowers. Producing abundant fish and lodging many birds and beasts, the lake is also a heaven for animals and plants, as well as rare medicinal materials including Chinese caterpillar fungus, fritillary and snow lotus. The natural pastureland around the lake offers ideal condition for animal husbandry. Wild animals, such as yaks, kiangs and foxes, can often be found in this area.

Lake Ra'og Coi: located in Paksho County in Chamdo Prefecture, the Lake Ra'og Coi is 3,850 meters above sea level with an area of 22 square kilometers, which makes it the largest lake in the southeast of Tibet. Fed by melting snow of the Lhagu Glacier, the lake is the source of Parlung Zangbo River, a major tributary of Yarlung Zangbo River. It is long and narrow, and crystal clear blue lake water, green pastureland around it and snowcapped mountains together represent a picturesque scene only in the south of the Yangtze River.

Yamdrok Tso Lake: Between Nakatse and Gongkar counties in Shannan Prefecture lies the Yamdrok Tso Lake, one of Tibet's four holy lakes, the other three being Namco, Mapam Yumco (Manasarovar Lake) and Lhamo Nhatso. Covering an area of more than 600 square kilometers, the lake is 4,441 meters above sea level. Its name means a lake of jade on grassland. As the name implies, in a bird's-eye view, it is like a big piece of sapphire inlaid in the mountains and is very beautiful. Wide in south and narrow in north, this lake has a quite irregular shoreline. The lakeshore area, with its rich water supply and lush grass, serves as an excellent grazing land for half fine-wool sheep.

Lake Conggo: Situated in lush primeval forest in Gongbogyamda County, Nyingchi Prefecture, the Lake Conggo is a holy lake of Nyingmapa, a religious sect of Lamaism. Its name means green water in local language. Resembling a crescent, the lake is only 36 square kilometers in area. However, thanks to its charms, the lake is often compared to a fairy maiden lying motionless on a green flannelette blanket. Autumn is the golden season when soft sunlight is seen through red leaves and the snow mountains mirror on the lake.

Lake Banggong: Covering an area of 604 square kilometers, the Lake Banggong extends from Rutog County of Ngari Prefecture of China to Kashmir. It is 150 kilometers long from east to west, making it the longest of its kind in China. What is remarkable about Lake Banggong is that it is filled with fresh water in its eastern half and with saltwater in its western half. The widest surface of the lake is 15 kilometers, but the narrowest is only 40 meters. There are a dozen of islands and islets on the lake, of which the most famous is the Bird Island with good ecological environment. It is only 300 meters in length and 200 meters in width, yet it is a habitat for thousands of various species of birds including bald-headed geese, brown-headed gulls, Black-headed Gull, Blue Throat, and others.

西藏自治区纳木错
Namco Lake, Tibet
Autonomous Region

1.2.西藏自治区雅鲁藏布江
Yarlung Zangbo, Tibet Autonomous Region

3.西藏自治区拉萨河
Lhasa River, Tibet Autonomous Region

1.西藏自治区然乌湖
Lake Ra'og Coi, Tibet Autonomous Region

2.3.西藏自治区纳木错
Namco Lake, Tibet Autonomous Region

1.2.西藏自治区羊卓雍错
   Yamdrok Tso Lake, Tibet
   Autonomous Region

3.西藏自治区班公错鸟岛
   Bird Island of Lake Banggong,
   Tibet Autonomous Region

4.西藏自治区错高湖风光
   Lake Conggo, Tibet Autonomous
   Region

1.西藏自治区错高湖秋色
**Lake Conggo in Autumn,
Tibet Autonomous Region**

2.西藏自治区昂仁湖
**Angren Lake, Tibet
Autonomous Region**

3.西藏自治区错那湖
**Cuona (CoNag) Lake, Tibet
Autonomous Region**

2

3

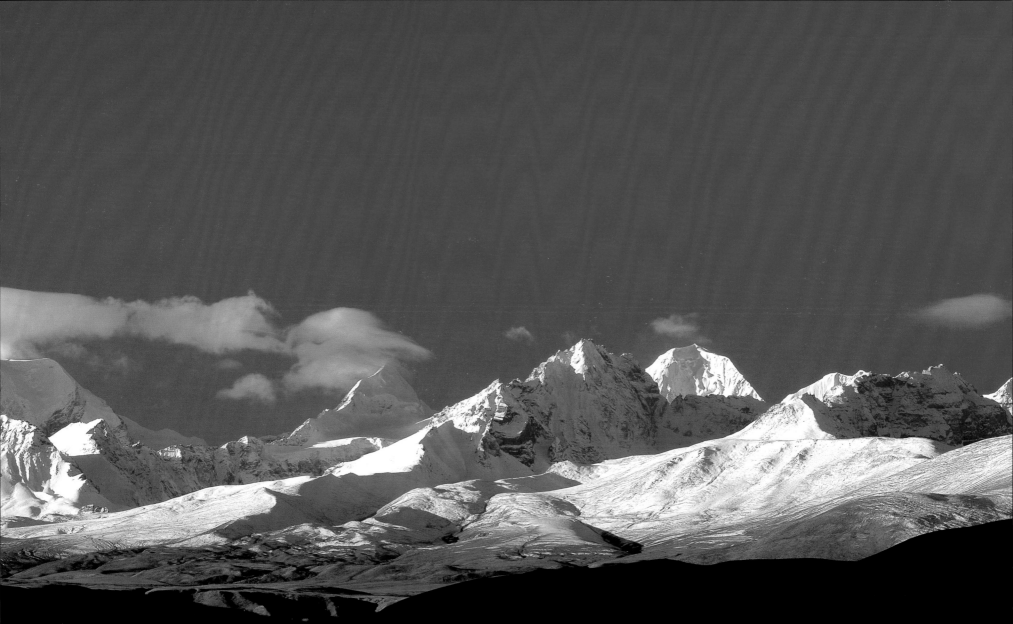

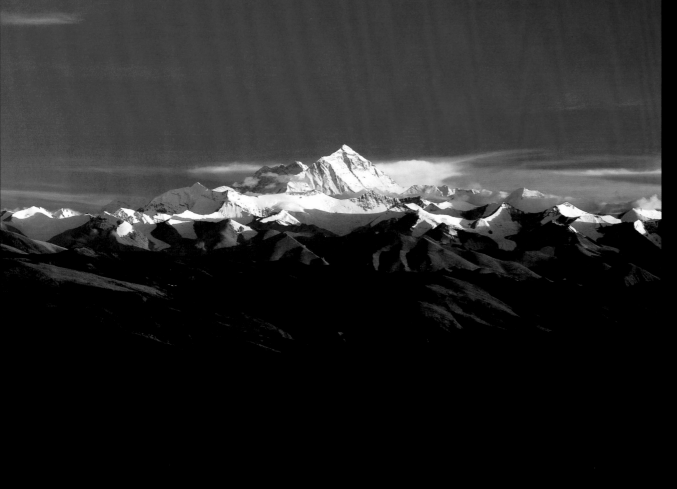

1. 西藏自治区珠穆朗玛峰
   Mt. Qomolangma, Tibet Autonomous
   Region

2. 西藏自治区喜马拉雅山
   The Himalayas, Tibet Autonomous Region

3. 西藏自治区希夏邦马峰
   Shisha Pangma (Gosainthan) Peak, Tibet
   Autonomous Region

4. 西藏自治区卓奥友峰
   Cho Oyu Peak, Tibet Autonomous Region

1

2

3

4

西藏自治区阿里札达土林
Earth Forest in Zanda County, Ngari,
Tibet Autonomous Region

西藏自治区阿里札达土林
**Earth Forest in Zanda County,
Ngari, Tibet Autonomous Region**

1. 西藏自治区念青唐古拉山
Nyainqentanglha Mountain, Tibet Autonomous Region

2. 西藏自治区冈仁波齐峰
Kangrinboqe Peak, Tibet Autonomous Region

3. 藏北草原风光
Scenery of Grassland of North Tibet

2

1.西藏自治区草原风光
Charming Scenery of Grassland in Tibet Autonomous Region

2.西藏自治区羊八井地热资源
Geothermal Resources of Yangbajain, Tibet Autonomous Region

3.西藏自治区林芝地区自然风光
Nature Scene of Nyingchi Area, Tibet Autonomous Region

4.西藏自治区纳木那尼峰
Naimona Nyi Peak, Tibet Autonomous Region

1−3陕西省华山风景名胜区
Huashan Mountain Scenic Resort,
Shaanxi Province

甘肃省鸣沙山
Echoing-Sand Hill, Gansu Province

甘肃省鸣沙山
Echoing-Sand Hill, Gansu Province

青海省青海湖鸟岛
Bird Isle of Qinghai Lake,
Qinghai Province

1. 青海省青海湖风光
   Attractive Qinghai Lake, Qinghai Province

2. 青海省日月山
   Riyue Mountain, Qinghai Province

3. 青海省草原风光
   Scenery of the Grassland in Qinghai Province

宁夏回族自治区沙坡头游览区
**Shapotou Tourist Zone, Ningxia
Hui Autonomous Region**

神奇大地——新疆
Mystic land: Xinjiang

新疆维吾尔自治区位于我国西北边疆，总面积160万平方千米，约占全国国土的六分之一，是中国面积最大的省份。在这片神奇的大地上，分布着众多奇伟瑰丽的景点，是令无数游人心驰神往的地方。

山脉：

新疆的主要地形特点是山脉与盆地相间排列，被喻为"三山夹二盆"。自治区内北部为阿尔泰山，南部有昆仑山系，中部横贯天山，将全区分割为南疆和北疆。南北各有一个巨大盆地，分别为塔里木盆地和准噶尔盆地。众多的雪山令这片寂静的雪域透着恢宏的气势，风光无比壮丽。

阿尔泰山脉：绵延于新疆北部，总长近2000千米，最高峰友谊峰海拔4373米，位于中、俄、蒙三国边界。阿尔泰山处于湿润的西风气流迎风面，森林密布、草场繁茂，是新疆畜牧业生产的重要基地。夏季草原碧绿，花海无边；冬季冰雪纯洁，一目千里，风光祷旎。

天山山脉：横亘新疆中部，峰峦重叠，气势雄伟，总长2500千米。天山最高峰托木尔峰海拔7435米，著名山峰还有汗腾格里峰（6995米）和博格达峰（5445米）。天山有发育良好的森林和草原，并分布着近7000条冰川，景色壮观，是天然的固体水库。融冰化雪汇集成200多条河流，滋润着天山南北的广阔绿洲。崇山峻岭之间，分布着众多土地肥沃、水草丰茂的盆地和谷地，形成了良好的山区天然草场，著名的有哈密盆地、吐鲁番盆地和伊犁河谷等。

昆仑山系：分布于塔里木沙漠南缘，巍峨高耸，平均海拔超过5000米，最高峰乔戈里峰海拔8611米，是世界第二高峰。此外，公格尔峰、公格尔九别峰和慕士塔格峰亦在这里拔地而起，直触云天，被称做"昆仑三雄"。其中，公格尔峰和公格尔九别峰，海拔分别为7719米和7595米，比肩而立，犹如一对亲密的姐妹；慕士塔格峰海拔7546米，悬挂有几十条银光闪闪的冰川，冰清玉洁，千姿百态，被誉为"冰山之父"。

湖泊：

新疆自治区内面积大于1平方千米的天然湖泊有100多个，水域面积约5500平方千米，其中著名的有：天池、博斯腾湖、赛里木湖、哈纳斯湖、艾丁湖、天鹅湖、卡拉库里湖等。

天池：处于博格达峰北侧，距阜康市约40千米。传说王母娘娘在此沐浴，故称瑶池。天池湖面海拔1980米，面积4.9平方千米，池深90米。湖水清澈如镜，晶莹如玉；四周雪峰环抱，云杉挺拔，塔松苍翠，绿草如茵，繁花似锦，风景秀丽，有"天山明珠"的

盛誉，是新疆最著名的风景名胜之一。

博斯腾湖：是我国最大的内陆淡水湖，位于巴音郭楞蒙古自治州。湖面海拔1048米，面积约980平方千米，水域辽阔，烟波浩淼，芦苇丛生，禽鸣鱼跃，一派江南水乡景色，有"西塞明珠"的美称，又被誉为"东方的夏威夷"。

赛里木湖：位于博尔塔拉蒙古自治州境内，又称"三台海子"。赛里木湖略呈椭圆形，水域面积450多平方千米，最深处91米，海拔2073米，是新疆最大的高山湖泊。湖岸林茂洞清，草深花繁，幕帐点点，炊烟袅袅，牛羊无数，骏马奔腾，构成一幅动人的牧场风景画。每年均在此举行蒙古族传统盛会"那达慕"。

哈纳斯湖：位于新疆北端，在蒙古语中意为"美丽富饶，神秘莫测"。湖面海拔1347米，面积约38平方千米。湖水清澈，雪峰倒映，湖周绿树墨林，艳花彩蝶，湖光山色，美不胜收。更为神奇的是，由于天气和角度的变化，湖水也随之变化成红、蓝、绿、白等颜色。到了金秋时节，湖畔层林尽染，万木争辉，五彩斑斓，如诗如梦，湖区宛如一个美丽的童话世界。

艾丁湖：是一个内陆咸水湖，在维吾尔语中意为月光湖，因湖中触目皆是洁白晶莹的盐结晶体，在阳光下闪闪发光，酷似寒夜晴空的月光，故名。艾丁湖位于吐鲁番盆地的"盆底儿"，湖面低于海平线155米，是中国第一、世界第二低地（仅次于死海）。

天鹅湖：位于巴音布鲁克草原之上，由大小不一的众多高山湖泊组成。这里雪山环抱，水草丰美，每年夏秋之际，数以万计的天鹅聚集于此，因此得名。

卡拉库里湖：位于慕士塔格峰脚下，海拔3600米，水光潋滟，映衬着巍峨神秘的雪山，尤显婀娜，景色迷人。

河流：

新疆境内冰川林立，河流纵横，是我国水资源最丰富的地区之一。其中，塔里木河全长2179千米，是中国最长的内陆河；伊犁河是新疆水量最大的河流；额尔齐斯河是我国惟一流入北冰洋的河流。河水流域绿草萋萋，阡陌纵横，风光优美，不知醉倒了多少游人。

沙漠：

新疆沙漠总面积43多万平方千米，占我国沙漠面积近60%。新疆境内，北部有古尔班通古特沙漠，南部有塔克拉玛干沙漠，此外还有白沙漠沙漠、库木库里沙漠、库姆塔格沙漠、哈密盆地沙漠和伊犁谷地沙漠，均为世界著名沙漠。其中，塔克拉玛干沙漠位于塔里木盆地，面积33.76万平方千米，是我国最大的

沙漠。沙丘连绵，沙浪起伏，沙漠宛如金黄色的浩瀚大海，气势雄浑，风光独特。

The northwest Chinese border region of Xinjiang is the largest province in China with an area of more than 1.6 million square kilometers, or one sixth of Chinese total territory. Xinjiang boasts boundless deserts, towering snowy mountains, dense forests, green range lands and crystal lakes. Its magnificent landscapes vary by season and have made Xinjiang a dreamland for countless tourists.

Mountains:

Xinjiang has three main mountains: Altay Mountain in north, Kunlun Mountains in south, and Tianshan Mountain in the center, which divides the region into north and south Xinjiang, each with a huge basin namely the Junggar Basin and the Tarim Basin. China's longest interior river, Tarim, the largest desert, Taklimakan, and the lowest basin, Turpan, are all in the region. Many lofty snowcapped mountains bestow the vast land surpassingly spectacular scenery.

Altay Mountain Range: Extending for about 2,000 kilometers, the Altay Mountain Range screens Xinjiang in the north. Its highest peak, Friendship Peak, rises 4,373 meters above sea level bordering Russia and Mongolia. The mountain facing the moist wind from the west boasts verdant forest and a lush growth of grass, making it one of the most important production bases of graziery in Xinjiang. In summer, the area features flourishing green grass and boundless sea of flowers, while a vast expanse of silver world in winter.

Tianshan Mountain Range: Running across the middle of Xinjiang, the snow-covered Tianshan Mountain Range is 2,500 kilometers long with imposing manner. The Tomur Peak is the highest peak of Tianshan with an elevation of 7,435 meters, and other famous peaks include Khan Tengri (6,995 meters), Bogda (5,445 meters) and so on. Besides, Tianshan possesses good conditions for forest and grassland growth, and nearly

7,000 glaciers turn it into a huge solid reservoir. Wide-spreading oases on both sides of the Tianshan are irrigated by more than 200 rivers which come from the melting snow in the mountains. Scattering among high mountains and towering peaks are many basins and valleys with fertile earth and lush pastures, such as Hami Basin, Turpan Basin and Ili Valley, ideal for stockbreeding.

Kunlun Mountain Range: Stretching along the southern fringe of the Tarim Desert, the lofty Kulun Mountain has an average altitude over 5,000 meters. The Chogo Ri Peak (K2) at an altitude of 8,611 meters is world's second highest peak behind the Mt. Qomolangma. What's more, the peaks of Kongur, Kongur-Tiube and Muztagata are known as the "Three Heroes of Kunlun" because of their astonishing height. The former two, standing shoulder by shoulder, are 7,719 meters and 7,595 meters high above sea level respectively, looking like a pair of sisters; the latter standing at an elevation of 7,546 meters is nicknamed the "Father of Ice Mountains", and tens of grand silver glaciers make it much mysterious.

Lakes:

Scattered on the vast land of Xinjiang are over 100 lakes more than 1 kilometer in area, and they cover a total of 5,500 square kilometers. The world famous lakes include Tianchi, Bosten Lake, Sayram Lake, Kanas Lake, Aiding Lake, Swan Lake, Kalakuli Lake and others.

Tianchi: Sprawling on the north slope of Bogda Peak and 40 kilometers from Fukang City, the Tianchi (Heavenly Lake) covers a total of 4.9 square kilometers with an altitude of 1,980 meters and an average depth of 90 meters. Legend has it that Wangmu Niangniang (Mother Goddess of Heaven) once bathed here, so it was formerly known as "Yaochi (Jade Lake)". Mirror-like lake surface, sparkling and crystal-clear water, snow-mantled peaks and sky-piercing spruces, verdant pines and a carpet of green grass, define Tianchi as a scenic place with prismatic splendor and win her the reputation of "Bright Pearl of Tianshan Mountain".

Bosten Lake: Located in Bayin'gholin Mongolia Autonomous Prefecture, the Bosten Lake is the largest inland freshwater lake in China, which is 1,048 meters in altitude and 980 square kilometers in area. With vast expanse of water and luxuriant vegetation, the lake reflects the beauty of the South China, and is also known as the "Oriental Hawaii". It is a large fishery where a variety of fish grow.

Sayram Lake: Also known as "Santai Haizi (literally, Three-Military-Dais Lake)", the lake lies in Botala Mongolia Autonomous Prefecture with an elevation of 2,073 meters above sea level, and is 91 meters deep at its deepest point. The oval-shaped lake covers an area of more than 450 square kilometers, which makes it the largest alpine lake in Xinjiang. The land around Sayram Lake is vast green grassland, forming a charming scene of pasture together with flourishing trees, crystal clear streams, blooming flowers, dotted yurts, whirling smokes, graze sheep and cattle, as well as galloping steeds. The Mongolian people celebrated the "Nadam Fair" beside the lake every year.

Kanas Lake: Lying in the north of Xinjiang, the Kanas Lake in the Mongolian language means a beautiful, rich and mysterious place. It is 1,347 meters high above sea level and covers an area of about 38 square kilometers. Kanas Lake is well-known for its color variations in different weathers or from different angles: dark green alternation with red, azure or milky white. It has varied and wonderful scenery in all seasons, but the autumn is considered the best time to go there, when it shows its brightest colors and most ardent beauty. In golden fall season, the snowcapped mountains mirror on the lake, the sky is high, and the mountain slopes and the forest which originally covered by green color then turns into a large patch of golden-yellow, blood-red, rose pink colored leaves. The whole mountain and plain get more sprayed perfumed with the autumn fragrance. All these create a fantasy world in fairyland.

Aiding Lake: An inland salt water lake, the Aiding means "Moonlight Lake" in Uygurian. It is covered by silvery white salt crystals and salt crusts shimmering on the dried-up lake bottom, hence the name. Located at the base of the Turpan Basin, it is seated 155 meters below sea level, which makes it the world's lowest land second only to the Dead Sea.

Swan Lake: Lying on the Bayanbulak Grassland, the Swan Lake is comprised of many a connected alpine lake. Embraced by snow mountains, the land features plenty of water and lush grass, and every year thousands of swans from many different species live, play and breed here, hence the name.

Kalakuli Lake: Located at the foot of Muztagata Peak, the Kalakuli Lake is 3,600 meters above sea level. With its sparkling water and glistening light of waves, the lake presents an incredible beautiful scene against lofty yet mysterious snowcapped mountains.

Rivers:

A forest of glaciers and crisscross rivers bestow Xinjiang abundant water resource. Among its rivers, the Tarim with a length of 2,179 kilometers is the longest continental river of China; the Ili River has the largest water yield in Xinjiang; and the Ertix River is the only river flows into the Arctic Ocean in China. With a luxuriant growth of grass, each of rivers features different charming scenery intoxicating countless tourists.

Deserts:

Xinjiang's desert area is more than 430,000 square kilometers, accounting for nearly 60 per cent of China's total desert area. In its territory there are such world famous deserts as Gurbantungut in north, Taklamakan in south, and Baishahu (White-Sand Lake) Desert, Kum-Tagh Desert, Kumukuli Desert, Hami Desert and Ili Valley Desert. Among them, the Taklamakan in the Tarim Basin is the largest in China, and covers an area of 337,600 square kilometers. They together constitute spectacular scenery with rolling sand dunes and rising and falling "sand waves".

新疆维吾尔自治区天山天池
Tianchi on the Tianshan Mountain,
Xinjiang Uygur Autonomous Region

新疆维吾尔自治区阿尔泰山
Altay Mountain, Xinjiang Uygur
Autonomous Region

新疆维吾尔自治区天山风光
Scenery of Tianshan Mountain,
Xinjiang Uygur Autonomous Region

1.新疆维吾尔自治区汗腾格里峰下昭苏军马场
Army Horse Ranch at the Foot of Khan Tengri Peak, Zhaosu County, Xinjiang Uygur Autonomous Region

2.新疆维吾尔自治区天山山脉
Tianshan Mountain Range, Xinjiang Uygur Autonomous Region

3.新疆维吾尔自治区那拉提旅游区
Nalati Tourist Zone, Xinjiang Uygur Autonomous Region

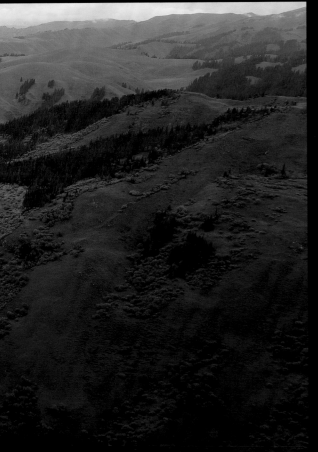

1. 新疆维吾尔自治区天山博格达峰
   Bogda Peak of the Tianshan Mountain Range, Xinjiang Uygur Autonomous Region

2. 新疆维吾尔自治区昆仑山公格尔峰
   Kongur Peak of the Kunlun Mountain Range, Xinjiang Uygur Autonomous Region

1

3.新疆维吾尔自治区昆仑山慕士塔格峰
Muztagata Peak of the Kunlun Mountain Range, Xinjiang Uygur Autonomous Region

4.新疆维吾尔自治区昆仑山公格尔九别峰
Kongur-Tiube Peak of the Kunlun Mountain Range, Xinjiang Uygur Autonomous Region

新疆维吾尔自治区天山天池
Tianchi on the Tianshan Mountain,
Xinjiang Uygur Autonomous Region

1.新疆维吾尔自治区天山天池
Tianchi on the Tianshan Mountain, Xinjiang Uygur Autonomous Region

2.新疆维吾尔自治区赛里木湖
Sayram Lake, Xinjiang Uygur Autonomous Region

3.新疆维吾尔自治区哈纳斯湖
Kanas Lake, Xinjiang Uygur Autonomous Region

1. 新疆维吾尔自治区巴音布鲁克天鹅湖
   Swan Lake on the Bayanbulak Grassland,
   Xinjiang Uygur Autonomous Region

2. 新疆维吾尔自治区巴音布鲁克草原夕照
   Bayanbulak Grassland at Sunset, Xinjiang
   Uygur Autonomous Region

3.新疆维吾尔自治区卡利库里湖
**Kalakuli Lake, Xinjiang Uygur
Autonomous Region**

4.新疆维吾尔自治区额尔齐斯河
**Ertix River, Xinjiang Uygur
Autonomous Region**

197

新疆维吾尔自治区塔克拉玛干沙漠
Taklamakan Desert in Xinjiang
Uygur Autonomous Region

新疆维吾尔自治区沙漠胡杨树
Diversiform-Leaved Poplars in
Xinjiang's Desert

1. 新疆维吾尔自治区魔鬼城
   Ghost Town, Xinjiang Uygur
   Autonomous Region

2. 新疆维吾尔自治区交河故城
   Ruins of Jiaohe City, Xinjiang
   Uygur Autonomous Region

3

4

3. 新疆维吾尔自治区石头城
**Stone City, Xinjiang Uygur
Autonomous Region**

4. 新疆维吾尔自治区高昌故城
**Ruins of Gaochang City, Xinjiang
Uygur Autonomous Region**

新疆维吾尔自治区五彩湾
Five-Hued Bay, Xinjiang Uygur Autonomous Region

新疆维吾尔自治区五彩湾
Five-Hued Bay, Xinjiang Uygur Autonomous Region

新疆维吾尔自治区库车峡谷
Kuche Valley, Xinjiang Uygur
Autonomous Region

新疆维吾尔自治区帕米尔高原风光
Scenery of the Pamirs Plateau,
Xinjiang Uygur Autonomous Region

North China

美丽的中国·北部

黑龙江省 Heilongjiang Province

吉林省 Jilin Province

辽宁省 Liaoning Province

河北省 Hebei Province

北京市 Beijing Municipality

天津市 Tianjin Municipality

山西省 Shanxi Province

内蒙古自治区 Inner Mongolia Autonomous Region

中国北部主要旅游景区间介：

八达岭：位于北京市西北部延庆县境内，距市区约60千米，由于地处交通要道，四通八达，故名。八达岭因盘亘于崇山峻岭之上的长城而驰名中外，同时，这里优美的自然风光也使长城别具风采。八达岭地区属于季风性气候，四季分明，风光迥异。春天，万物复苏，生机勃勃，漫山遍野的杏花、山桃花争奇斗艳，吐露着迷人的芳香；夏天，微风轻拂，空气湿润，绿树成阴，雄伟的长城宛如一条巨龙游弋在绿色的海洋之中；秋天，天空如碧，林木斑斓，层林尽染；冬天，冰雕玉砌，银装素裹，一派北国风光。景区内山势雄奇，地貌复杂，动植物景观丰富，具有优美的生态环境。积淀深厚的历史文化与大自然互相融合，组成了八达岭无穷的魅力。

香山：香山位于北京市西郊，占地160万平方米。主峰海拔557米，因形似香炉，故名"香炉峰"。峰虽不高，地势险发，俗称"鬼见愁"。香山以"翠"取胜，山奇水秀，草木紫茂，环境幽雅，有各类树木26万余株，其中，一、二级古树、名木5800余株，植被覆盖率达96%以上，是春游踏青、夏季避暑、秋观红叶、冬赏雪景的好去处。久负盛名的香山红叶，早在金代就已经成为文人墨客争相歌咏的景物，清乾隆皇帝所定的"二十八景"中的"绚秋林"，就是此景。每年九、十月份，秋高气爽，满山红叶，层林尽染，煞是好看，是游人登山欣赏秋色奇景的好季节。香山还有名胜古迹数十处。其中，著名的有：燕京八景之一的"西山晴雪"和碧云寺、双清别墅、昭庙、见心斋、香山寺遗址等。

承德避暑山庄：承德市位于河北省东北部。这里峰峦挺拔，土地平旷，树木葱郁，河流萦绕，自然景色秀丽，气候凉爽宜人，既富有北国风光，又兼具江南景色。300多年前就被清朝康熙皇帝青睐，在此处建成了中国现存最大的皇家园林——避暑山庄。山庄虽由人作，宛若天成，历代帝王在修葺时也精心设计，并巧妙地运用了艺术手法，师法自然，融于自然，表现自然，又高于自然，充分展示了人与自然的和谐统一。避暑山庄分为宫殿区和苑景区两大部分，后者占去了山庄绝大部分面积。建造者充分地利用了山庄得天独厚的自然条件，远山近黛、远湖近水均被成功地借入园内成景，山取水秀，水得山幽；而宫宇建筑，巧借自然，既不夺自然之美，又更添精巧之效，可谓相得益彰。避暑山庄是皇家建筑的经典之作，亦是无与伦比的自然美景。1994年，避暑山庄连同雄踞在周围的外八庙一起，被联合国教科文组织列入《世界遗产名录》。

北戴河：位于河北省秦皇岛市西南15千米处。东起鹰角石，西至戴河口，全长10千米，海滨景色优美，沙软滩平，海水清澈，是中国著名的避暑胜地。北戴河背依联峰山，其由三座松林覆盖的山峰连绵而成，远望似莲蓬，因此又称为莲蓬山。山上松柏葱郁，怪石、幽径、曲桥、亭塔，错落其间，相映成趣。位于北戴河海滨东北的鹰角石鸽子窝，是眺望大海，观赏日出的旅游胜地。此处傍海悬崖，有一高约20米的巨石，形似鹰集，故名。又因鸽鱼每于春夏

原纵横，常有野鸽于栖息于此，故又名鸽子窝。

坝上草原：位于河北省北部，因在华北平原和内蒙古高原交接的地方，地势陡然升高呈阶梯状，因此称为"坝上"。坝上草原东起承德市围场满族蒙古族自治县，西至张家口市张北县，总面积350平方千米，山峦起伏，森林茂密，草木丰美，溪流纵横，是各种动物繁育的天然栖息地。盛夏之时，这里气候凉爽，一望无际的大草原开满了各种各样的鲜花，姹紫嫣红，如同花的海洋；金秋时节，苍山滴翠，山林茂密，万山红遍，野果飘香；隆冬腊月，展现出"千里冰封，万里雪飘，山舞银蛇，原驰蜡象"的雄伟壮观的北国风光。无垠草原、远山峻岭、蓝天白云，在不同季节散发出不同的魅力，犹如一幅幅优美的油画，向人们展示着这塞北灵秀神奇的草原景色。

苍岩山：位于河北省石家庄市井陉县东南，距石家庄市70千米，海拔1000余米，是国家级重点风景名胜区之一。大自然的鬼斧神工使苍岩山中心地带形成了奇异的绝壁断崖及优越的生态环境。山上古木参天，层峦叠翠，气候温和，景色迷人，以"楼绝、檀奇、山雄、谷幽、林秀"著称，共有十六佳景，是冀中地区一处旅游、观光、避暑胜地。这里不仅自然风光优美，而且宗教寺庙众多，主要的有福庆寺、书院、万仙堂、公主祠、桥楼殿、玉皇顶、峰回轩、藏经楼等。其中，桥楼殿最为著名，是我国三大悬空寺之一。福庆寺则因隋炀帝之女南阳公主曾在此削发为尼而知名。

壶口瀑布：位于山西省吉县西南25千米处、黄河之中。黄河奔流至此，突然被两岸山峦夹峙收成一束，河水飞泻跌落，如万马奔腾直入河沟，惊涛怒吼，波浪翻腾，咆哮之声震耳欲聋，形成气势恢宏的瀑布奇观。古人留下了"天下黄河一壶收"、"十里河滩闻惊雷"、"秋风卷起千层浪，晚日迎来万丈红"等许多著名的诗句。这里，自古即有"旱地行船"、"飞鸟难渡关"之说。壶口上游河水流泻迅猛，船行至此即靠岸停泊，由船夫拉到岸上，并一直在陆地上将船拖拽到瀑布下游水流平缓的岸边，再推入河中；而由于瀑布呼啸震天，云烟弥漫，鸟飞至此，惊吓得不敢越过，可见瀑布的惊险、磅礴。壶口瀑布，景因时变：春天，冰开雪化，冰凌抛落，浪花四溅，如山崩地裂；夏秋，雨水充沛，浊浪腾空，如从天降，洪波怒号，气贯长虹；冬季，银装素裹，冰雕玉琢，状如凝脂，分外妖娆。

北岳恒山：恒山位于山西省浑源县境内，为五岳之中的北岳。传说，舜帝北巡时，见恒山山势雄伟挺拔，因此将其封为"北岳"。恒山自然风光天趣盎然，人文景观独具魅力，自古以来就是帝王、墨客历游之处，留下大量的诗词碑刻。恒山号称108峰，东西绵亘150余千米，以险峰、峭壁、奇石、涌泉、林海、寺观引人入胜，被誉为"塞北第一山"。恒山分为东、西两峰；东为天峰岭，西为翠屏峰。双峰对峙，山势险峻，自古即为兵家必争之地。天峰岭，海拔2017米，为恒山最高峰，陡峭的北坡之上遍布苍苍苍的松树林，南坡则建有众多古代帝王祭祀北岳修建的庙

子道观，现在尚存悬空寺、飞石屈、会仙府、九天宫等多处。恒山风景区风光秀丽，是国务院公布的第一批国家重点风景名胜区之一。

五台山：位于山西省忻州地区五台县，是中国四大佛教名山之一。因该山由望海峰、锦绣峰、翠岩峰、挂月峰和叶斗峰五座山峰组成，峰顶平坦如台，故名。最高峰北台海拔3058米，素称"华北屋脊"。这里，峰峦连绵，山岳交错，沟壑纵横，谷河漫流，林木荤翠，风光如画。因夏季气候凉爽，五台山又有"清凉台"之誉。五台山在东汉年间即有寺庙建筑，现存寺庙47处，所建年代及形制各不相同，是中国保存寺庙最多、最完整的佛教名山，也是中国佛教活动的重要场所之一。著名的有显通寺、塔院寺、万佛阁、菩萨顶等。苍翠挺拔的松柏、叠翠险峻的峰崖、幻化莫测云海，以及金碧辉煌的殿宇楼台，赋予了五台山无穷的魅力。

响沙湾：位于鄂尔多斯库布齐沙漠北缘、内蒙古自治区达拉特旗境内，距包头市45千米，以沙漠景观和响沙奇观为主要特色。响沙湾沙丘高达90米，沙坡斜度约45度，呈月牙形。登到沙丘顶端往下滑时，就会听到沙子发出的如同击鼓、吹号的鸣鸣声。若是三五人同时下滑，则其声如洪钟，又似飞机的轰鸣，使人感到神奇有趣。千百年来，人们惊奇于沙丘的响声，赋予它许多美丽的传说。

库布齐沙漠为内蒙古三大沙漠之一，总面积达1600多平方千米。库布齐是蒙古语，汉语为"弓弦"的意思。沙漠以流动沙丘为主，约占80%左右，一般高10～15米向西流动，大有与毛乌素沙地会合的趋势。大漠一望无际美不胜收，给人如诗如梦的感受和无限的遐想空间。如恰好有驼队在沙丘缓行，还可听到悦耳的驼铃声。游客置身其中，远离城市的喧嚣，感受到一份让心灵宁静的温馨。还可骑骆驼、观看民族歌舞。

呼伦湖：又称达赉湖，是中国著名的淡水湖之一，也是内蒙古第一大湖。该湖位于呼盟满洲里东45千米处，总面积2339平方千米，水深8米左右，被誉为"呼伦贝尔草原的一颗明珠"。呼伦湖区气候凉爽，碧波万顷，景色宜人，是夏季旅游、避暑的胜地。该湖属富营养型湖泊，水产资源丰富，鸟类栖息环境佳良，为观鸟赏鱼的绝佳去处。初步统计，呼伦湖地区共有鸟类200多种，主要有天鹅、雁、鸭、鹭等，堪称一座硕大的鸟类博物馆。此外，阳光浴、湖沙浴、湖畔垂钓、乘船游湖等游览项目会使人乐而忘返，还可以在湖边品尝鲜嫩可口、营养丰富的全鱼宴。冬季可观赏冰下捕鱼，别有一番情趣。

呼伦贝尔草原：位于内蒙古呼伦贝尔盟，是中国北方游牧民族的发源地之一，因其旁边的呼伦湖和贝尔湖而得名

伦和贝尔在蒙古语中分别为水獭和雌水獭的意思。古代这两个大湖盛产水獭，因此得名。呼伦贝尔草原总面积约约0万平方千米，为中国最大的草原。草原大部分是平缓的原野，绿茵如毯，一望无垠，河流纵横，明镜般的湖泊星罗棋布。微风拂过，鲜花烂漫，牛羊成群，蒙古包点缀其间，犹如绿海中的白帆，风光极为绮丽，令人如痴如梦，心旷神怡，可充分领略"天苍苍，野茫茫，风吹草低见牛羊"的意境。

千山：位于辽宁省鞍山市东南，距市中心约20千米处，是长白山的一个支脉。从空中俯视，似千朵莲花绽放在辽东半岛的腹地，因此又名千朵莲花山。古人有诗："欲向青天数花朵，九百九十九芙蓉"，即是对千山的绝唱。千山为国家级风景名胜区，面积约为72平方千米，林木葱茏，植被丰富，自然风光十分秀丽。千山风景区以峰秀、石峭、谷幽、松奇、花盛、庙古、佛高著称。其中，"佛高"指的是一尊由整座山峰形成的天然弥勒佛坐像。大佛高70余米，肌体丰满，神态悠然，形象逼真，栩栩如生，端坐在一朵莲花中，令人莫不感叹大自然的神奇。近年，在大佛脚下还发掘出明清两代的供器，这里成为东北地区的佛教圣地。

笔架山：位于辽宁省西部渤海辽东湾西岸，距锦州市约35千米，是近海一个连陆山岛。岛屿面积1平方千米，海拔78米，因岛上山峰形如笔架而得名。小岛看似孤立，实际有一条神奇的"天桥"，使它与陆地紧密相连。"天桥"全长1600余米，宽约27米，是一条潮汐冲击而成的天然通道，随着潮水的涨落时隐时现，堪称奇观。每当落潮时，海水便慢慢向两边退去，一条蜿蜒的蛟龙浮现在海中，直通笔架山，很是神奇。笔架山是观赏海上日出的绝佳之处，日出时分，霞光瑞气，照彻天地，红日冉冉，光芒万丈，异常壮观。岛上还有吕祖亭、五母宫、三清阁等古迹。

镜泊湖：位于黑龙江省东南部宁安市境内，距牡丹江市110千米。它是由于大约1万年前火山喷发，熔岩堵塞了牡丹江河道堰塞而成。全湖面积95平方千米，南北长近50千米，最宽处6千米，蜿蜒曲折，呈S形。镜泊湖是中国最大的高山湖之一，湖面如镜，湖水清澈，湖周群山环抱，湖岛星罗棋布，风光尤为绮旎，被喻为"北方的西湖"，每年吸引着众多的游客来此度假休闲、消夏避暑。湖区自然天成的吊水楼瀑布、珍珠门、大小孤山等八景更是迷人，流传着许多美丽的神话故事和传说。其中，吊水楼瀑布位于镜泊湖北端，是我国著名的瀑布之一。瀑布终年不息，流幅40米，落差达25米。飞瀑直泻，水雾蒸腾，彩虹迭起，涛声雷动，非常壮观。

大兴安岭：美丽富饶的大兴安岭林区，位于我国的最北边垂，东连绵延千里的小兴安岭，西依呼伦贝尔大草原，北与俄罗斯隔江相望，南达土地肥沃的松嫩平原。境内山峦叠嶂，林海苍茫，气势雄浑。大兴安岭是我国面积最大的现代化林区，总面积约8.5万平方千米，林木蓄积量5亿立方米。在浩瀚的绿色海洋中繁衍生息着寒温带马鹿、刺

麋、梅花鹿、狍子、野猪、雪兔、棕熊、紫貂、野鸡、天鹅等400余种珍禽异兽和1000多种植物，此外还有鲟鲤鱼、细鳞、江雪鱼等众多的冷水鱼类生活在纵横其间的河湖中，是我国高纬度地区不可多得的野生动、植物乐园。当地人用"棒打狍子瓢舀鱼，野鸡飞到饭锅里"来形容这里的野生动物资源实在不为过。春来百花吐芳，夏至苍翠欲滴，秋到层林尽染，冬临皎洁晶莹，大兴安岭四季景异，极具诗意，是集观光、狩猎、垂钓、漂流于一体的综合性旅游景区。

五大连池：位于黑龙江省北部的五大连池市，是我国著名的火山旅游胜地。200多年前火山喷发，熔岩堵塞了当年的河道，形成了这五个串珠样的、互相联接的熔岩堰塞湖，统称五大连池。景区内堪称山秀、石怪、水幽、泉奇、老黑山、火烧山等14座锥体火山耸立在五个湖泊周围，植被葱郁，山环水抱，交相辉映，蔚为壮观；千姿百态的熔岩散布其间，惟妙惟肖，令人目不暇接。此外，这里盛产的矿泉水，含有多种人体必需的微量元素，具有治病、防病和保健的功效。奇特的火山风光、丰富完整的火山地貌和疗效显著的矿泉"圣水"，使五大连池享有"火山公园"和"天然火山博物馆"的美誉，是游览观光、休闲疗养和科学考察的理想之所。

Major scenic areas in the North China are as follows:

Badaling: Badaling is located in Yanqing County, Beijing Municipality, more than 60 kilometers northwest from Beijing proper. As its name implies, it gives access to every direction. This area is known all over the world for the Great Wall sprawling on the summit of high mountain ridges, and the beautiful natural scenery adds extraordinarily charm to the Great Wall. Badaling has a monsoon climate marked by four distinct seasons with widely different views. In spring, the place is taken over by a riot of flowers such as apricot and mountain peach, which contend in beauty and fascination and send off sweet fragrance; in summer, the wind blows gentle and soothing, air is moist, and the dragon-like Great Wall in this green ocean, offers a spectacular scene; in autumn, the mountains towering against blue sky are dyed crimson by autumn leaves; and in winter the entire place puts on a thick snow mantle. Featuring awesome mountain and complex landforms, Badaling has a wonderful ecological environment and is home to a rich variety of flora and fauna. Profound historical and cultural intensions, as well as attractive natural scenery together form Badaling's unique charm.

Xiangshan: The Xiangshan (Fragrant Hill) in northwestern Beijing covers an area of 1.6 million square meters. The Xianglufeng (Incense Burner Peak) is the summit of the Fragrant Hills with a height of 557 meters. It looks like an incense burner at a distance hence the name. Though it is not very tall by all standards, it seems to be precarious due to the plunging ravines on both sides, which gains it a nickname "Ghost Worrying Peak". The area has a dense forest with 260,000 trees of various species, including 5,800 Grade A and B ancient trees. Ninety per cent of the hills are covered by trees. Well-known for its beautiful scenery, the Xiangshan is attractive all year round, a nice place for spring outing, a resort to escape the summer heat, and a choice to admire the maple leaves in autumn and snow in winter. The maple leaves in golden autumn has attracted numerous visitors since the Jin Dynasty. Xuanqiulin (Gorgeous Forest in Autumn), one of Qianlong's 28 scenes at Xiangshan, indicates it. The park looks its seasonal best in September and October, when the sky is high and the air brisk and the entire hill is covered with flaming maple leaves. There are many places of interest on the Xiangshan, and the most famous are the Xishanqingxue (West Hills Shimmering in Snow, one of the Eight Great Views of Yanjing), the Biyunsi (Temple of Azure Clouds), Shuang Qing (Double Clear Springs) Villa, Zhaomiao (Luminous Temple, or Sakyamuni's Temple), Jianxinzhai (Studio of Introspection) and Ruins of Xiangshansi (Temple of Fragrant Hill).

Chengde Mountain Resort: Lying is northeast of Hebei Province, the city of Chengde boasts beautiful natural scenery and pleasant climate. The magnificent mountains, vast expense of field, luxuriant trees, crystalline streams form the typical landscape of north China, yet containing elements of scenery in the lower Yangtze valley. As early as 300 years ago, the land found favor in Qing Emperor Kangxi's eyes and then he wasted no time in building the Mountain Resort, the largest imperial garden extant in China. Each of the emperors paid more attention to the construction of the resort and laid out exquisitely. They learned from nature merged the landscapes into nature, expressed nature and made the man-made landscapes finer than nature. The garden shows great harmony of man and nature and extremely displays the essence of art of Chinese classi

河北省坝上草原
Bashang Grassland
Hebei Province

al gardening. It looks like being made by nature. The resort itself falls into two parts: the palaces and the gardens, the latter taking up the overwhelming majority of its territory. Making full use of the terrain, the architect sought to use diverse forms of buildings and their supplements to exhibit breath-taking natural beauty. Mountain and lakes, both in and out of the resort are borrowed to enhance the beauty of the Mountain Resort and brings about strong space effect. The lakes bring the landscape a sense of gracefulness, while the mountains make the water scenery much tranquil; and they set off with the architectural structures into a harmonious entirety. The entire resort is a veritable museum of ancient Chinese garden culture and horticulture, as well as an unmatched natural scenery. In 1994, the Mountain Resort, together with the Eight Outer Temples surrounding it, was inscribed on the World Heritage List by the UNESCO.

Beidaihe Beach Resort: About 15 kilometers south-west of Qinhuangdao City in Hebei Province, the Beidaihe Beach Resort is a famous scenic summer resort. It stretches 10 kilometers from the Yingjiaoshi (Eagle Corner Rock) in the east to the mouth of the Daihe River in the west. Its charm lies mostly in the soft sands, gentle beach and clear seawater. The environment around Beidaihe is also beautiful. Mt. Lianfeng (Linking Peaks), backing onto the beach, has three peaks covered by abundant green pines and cypresses. Viewing from distant, it resembles a seed-pod of the lotus, so it is nicknamed the Mountain of Lotus-Seedpod. Lush vegetation, strange stones, deco-rated pavilions, secluded paths, ancient pagodas and winding bridges cover the mountain and make it unique and appealing. "Dove Nest" of the Yingjiaoshi is one of the most popular attractions, where visitors can enjoy watching the sun-rising and powerfully energetic ocean. The Yingjiaoshi takes its name from a 20-meter-high rock, which by sea, like an eagle. And wild doves often nestle in crevices on the surface of rock, so it is also called the Dove Nest.

Bashang Grassland: Lying in the north of Hebei Province, the Bashang Grassland is located at the junction of the North China Plain and Inner Mongolia Plateau. The grassland extends northward and sud-denly rises, forming a step-like shape, hence the name, which means grassland on the dam in Chinese. Stretching from Weichang Manchu and Mongolia Autonomous County of Chengde City in the east to Zhangbei County of Zhangjiakou City in the west, the

Bashang Grassland covers a total of 350 square kilometers, featuring rising mountains, dense forest, plentiful grass, crisscross springs and streams. It is a paradise for animals. In midsummer, it is cool, and flowers of various colors burst into full blossom, turn-ing the vast grassland into a sea of flowers. In autumn, the mountains are covered with green and dense forests, fruits send off fragrance, and viewed in distance, red maple leaves are like flaring flame. In the depth of winter, it becomes a world of ice and snow and shows the North scene. The boundless grassland, plus the imposing mountains and white clouds in the blue sky, constitutes to different oil paintings varying with the season changing and mag-netizes visitors with its amazing beauty.

Cangyan Mountain: Situated in southeast of Jingxing County in Shijiazhuang City, Hebei Province, the Cangyan Mountain is 70 kilometers away from Shijiazhuang. More than 1,000 meters in elevation, it features marvelous bold cliffs made by nature and favorable ecological environment, and is one of na-tional important scenic resorts. Covered with luxuri-ant ancient trees, the rolling mountain has mild cli-mate and charming scenery, and is famous for its five wonders—wonderful towers, rare wingceltis, impos-ing peaks, secluded valleys and beautiful forests re-spectively—and 16 unique scenic spots. It is a popu-lar mountain resort. Beyond its picturesque landscape, it is also renowned for many religion architectural clusters on the mountain, such as Fuqingsi (Fortune Celebration Temple), Shuyuan (Academy), Wanxian-tang (Hall of Ten-Thousand Immortals), Gongzhuci (Memorial Temple of Princess), Qiaoloudian (Hall of Bridging Tower), Yuhuangding (Summit of Jade Emperor), Fenghuixuan (Hall of Winding Ridges) and Cangjinglou (Tower for Storing Sutra). Of them, Qiaoloudian, one of three suspending temples in China, is the most famous. Fuqingsi houses a particu-larly fine statue of Princess Nanyang, allegedly the eldest daughter Emperor Yang of the Sui Dynasty (581-618) who became a nun here.

Hukou Waterfall: The Hukou (Pot Spout) Waterfall on the Yellow River is situated at 25 kilometers west of Jixian County, Shanxi Province. When the Yellow River flows to the place, the water of the river is squeezed by mountains on both banks into a narrow gorge like the spout of a pot and rush rapidly, forming the grand waterfall. It is known for the rapid speed of the water and as the thunderous sound. Poets and scholars of the past dynasties came here and left behind many

famous poems of admiration and appreciation of the spectacular scenery. The most famous descriptions are: The Yellow River under heaven is contained into a pot; Five-kilometers-long benchland is shocked by the tremendous noise; The Autumn wind rolls up thousands of layers of waves, and the setting sun dyed lofty waterfall red. The waterfall is so tremendous that in the past, people had to drag the boats onto land to pass through this section of the Yellow River. Even the flying birds don't dare to pass it because of the mist and spray, as well as the roaring of waterfall. The charming scenery of Hukou Waterfall varies with seasons. When the snow and ice melt in spring, the waterfall pours down with icicles and spindrifts, like heaven falling and earth cracking; in summer and autumn during flood season, the yellow river comes down in torrents, with breathtakingly beautiful splashes and deafening sound; while in winter, the frozen water is in silver mantle, like being carved elaborately.

Hengshan Mountain: The Hengshan Mountain is lo-cated in Hunyuan County of Shanxi Province in north-ern China. It is the Northern Mountain of the Five Sacred Mountains. Legend has it that when he toured northern domain some 4,000 years ago, Emperor Shun was so impressed by the sight of Hengshan Mountain that he proclaimed it the "North Mountain". Since then, it has been attracting many emperors, celebri-ties and travelers by its natural sceneries and man-made landscaping, and quite a lot of stone inscrip-tions of poems were left there. Boasting 108 peaks and spanning 150 kilometers, Hengshan is famous for steep ridges, splendid peaks, peculiar-shaped rocks, gushing fountains, forests of trees, as well as ancient temples, which constitutes a beautiful landscape. The mountain enjoys the reputation of "The First Mountain Guarding the North Borders", which depicts its magnitude and wonder. The moun-tain consists of two peaks: the Tianfengling (Heavenly Peak Ridge) in the east and the Cuipingfeng (Emerald Screen Peak) in the west. Tianfengling, 2,017 meters above sea level, is the highest peak. Its abrupt north-ern slope is covered with verdant pine trees, while located on its southern slope are 10-odd temples and monasteries built by ancient kings and emperors to worship their ancestors, including Xuankongsi (Midair

Temple), Feishika (Flying Stone Grottoes), Huixiannu Mansion of Meeting Immortals), Jiutiangong (Nine-Heaven Palace) and others. The two peaks stand facing each other and form a precipitous natural barrier, making it a place contested by all strategists. Hengshan Mountain Scenic Spots was inscribed on the first list of major scenic areas and historical sites in the country proclaimed by the State Council.

Wutai Mountain: Located in Wutai County of Xinzhou Prefecture in Shanxi Province, the Wutai Mountain is one of the Four Most Famous Buddhist Mountains in China. It consists of five terrace-like peaks—Wanghai (Watching Sea), Jinxiu (Brocade), Cuiyan (Green Rock), Guiyue (Hanging Moon) and Yedou (God of North and Big Dipper) respectively, hence the name. The highest peak, Yedou, has an altitude of 3,058 meters, so it is nicknamed as the "Roof of North China". The Wutai Mountain features picturesque landscape, which is constituted of rolling peaks and ridges, crisscross gullies and ravines, winding rivers and streams, as well as luxuriant forest. The mountain is cool and pleasant in summer, and has been regarded as an ideal place for escaping summer heat since ancient times, which wins it a nickname: Qingliangtai (Cool and Pleasant Terrace). As early as the Eastern Han Dynasty, there were temples built here. The 47 temples and monasteries existing at present, built in different dynasties and in various styles, have turned the Wutai Mountain into a center of activities for Chinese Buddhist. Of them, the most famous ones include Xiantongsi (Temple of Displaying Magical Power), Tayuansi (Dagoba-Courtyard Temple), Wanfoge (Pavilion of Ten-Thousand Buddhas) and Pusading (Summit of Budhisattva). The tall and green pines and cypresses, piled verdure of steep peaks, mysterious and constantly changing sea of clouds and splendid architectural structures bestow the Wutai Mountain endless charms.

Resonant Sand Gorge: Located at the northern edge of Ordos Kubqi Desert in the Dalad Banner, Inner Mongolia Autonomous Region, the Resonant Sand Gorge is about 45 kilometers from Baotou City, featuring desert scenery and singing sand. It has a crescent-shaped dune rising up to 90 meters high with a slope of about 45 degrees. When people climb up to the top of the sand dune and slide down, they are able to hear the sounds which are similar to sound of a drum-roll, or the noise made by cars or planes. Resonant sand is still a mysterious phenomenon beyond people's explanation, so people bestow it many beau-

tiful legends and tales.

The Kubqi Desert means bowstring in Mongolian. It is one of the three large deserts in Inner Mongolia and covers an area more than 16,000 square kilometers. Generally speaking, the sand dunes of the Kubqi are 10 to 15 meters high and moving dunes make up 80% of the total area. Some of the sand dunes on the edge of the desert move so fast that they are about meet the Maowusu sand land in the west. The boundless desert offers unmatched and splendid scenery, and brings tourist poetic and dream-like feeling as well as unlimited imagination. If there is a camel train there, you also could hear sweet sound of camel bells. You can also ride a camel and enjoy the performance of local dances and songs to learn about the local customs and manners.

Lake Hulun: Lake Hulun, also called the Lake Dalai, is one of the most famous freshwater lakes of China. It is the largest lake in Inner Mongolian and is reputed as a pearl on the Hulun Buir Grassland. Situated in the place 45 kilometers east of Manchuli City of the Hulun Buir League, the Lake is 8 meters deep and covers an area of 2,339 square kilometers. The area is a summer resort with a mild cold climate and picturesque landscape. The lake is a clean paradise with a huge variety of wildlife, from fishes to waterfowl. Observing and appreciating birds and fish here will be a great pleasure for the tourists. According to incomplete statistics, for annually the lake is home to over 200 migrating bird species, including swans, gulls, wild ducks and egrets. It does be a large bird museum. Additionally, sunbathing, lake sand bathing, fishing, going boating, along with other activities, often make the visitors in such a high spirit that they find it hard for them to say "good-bye" to this beautiful place. Besides these, they can also have a "complete feast of fish", made of fresh, tender, delicious and nutritious fish in instantly captured from the lake. Observing how people here catch fish under the ice in winter is another attraction for the visitors.

Hulun Buir Grassland: Located in the League with the same name of the Inner Mongolia Autonomous Region, the Hulun Buir Grassland is one of the birthplaces of the ancient nomadic people and hunting tribes in north China. It is named after two lakes: Hulun and Buir. The former in Mongolian language means otter, while the latter male otter, because both of lakes teemed with otters in ancient times. The Hulun Buir Grassland covers an area of 100,000 square kilometers, ranking first in China. Covered with ver-

dant grass and colorful flowers, the gently grassland stretches to the horizon, crisscrossed by rivers and studded with mirror-like lakes. Against the blue sky and white clouds horses gallop, presenting the heroic bearing of the herdsmen. Just as a folk song describes: "The boundless grassland lies, Beneath the boundless skies. When the winds blow, And grass bends low, Flocks of sheep and herds of cattle will show."

Qianshan Mountain: The Qianshan Mountain, located southeast of Anshan, 20 kilometers from city proper, is the branch range of Changbai (Ever White) Mountain. Looking down from the air, the mountain likes a thousand lotus flowers in bloom on the hinder land of Liaodong Peninsula, so it is also nicknamed Qianduolianhua, which means a thousand lotus-flowers in Chinese. An ancient poem describes the scene, "I intend to count the flowers in the sky, only 999 lotus flowers meet my eye." Covering an area of 72 square kilometers, the Qianshan Mountain is densely wooded, and abounds in flora and fauna, and is a national scenic resort. It boasts grateful peaks, steep rocks, secluded valleys, strange shaped pines, blooming flowers, ancient temples, as well as giant Buddha. Of them, the giant Buddha is a nature sitting statue of the Maitreya Buddha forming by a peak. With a height of 70 meters, the lifelike statue has a well shaped body and looks perfectly relaxed. The place has since become a holy land of Buddhism in northeast China. And many sacrificial utensils of the Ming and Qing dynasties were discovered at the foot of the peak.

Bijia Mountain: The Bijia (Pen-Rest) Mountain is a mountain island near the western shore of the Liaodong Bay in western Liaoning, 35 kilometers from the city of Jinzhou. The peaks on the island resemble a pen-rest, hence the name. Although looked isolated, the island is actually linked with land by a natural bridge created by tide, a magical bridge known as "heavenly bridge". Heavy fog always surrounds the island, making it look mysterious. The Bijia Mountain covers an area of only 1 square kilometers and rises 78 meters above sea level, and the bridge is more than 1,600 meters in length and 27 meters in width. It zigzags its way towards the island, and looks like a

beautiful dragon. This "heaven-made" bridge that appears and disappears as the tide rises and falls is an unusual wonder in the world. Walking along it is truly pleasurable. The island is also famous for its spectacular sunrise and sunset views. The beautiful sunshine silhouettes the mountain, bathing everything in golden colors. Built on the island are such historical sites as Luzuting (Pavilion of Patriarch Lu Dongbin), Wumugong (Palace of Five Goddesses) and Sanqingge (Tower of Three Purities).

Jingpo Lake: Lying in Ning'an City in the southeast of Heilongjiang Province and 110 kilometers from Mudanjiang City, the Jingpo Lake came into being some 10,000 years ago when major volcanic eruption in the region led to blocking of the course of the Mudan (Peony) River. It covers a total of 95 square kilometers with a length of nearly 50 kilometers, and the widest point reaches to 6 kilometers. Winding its way, the lake is in the shape of the letter "S". One of the largest alpine lakes in China, the Jingpo Lake is embraced by rolling mountains and dotted with isles, and features mirror-like surface. The lake water is so clear that you can see bottom through it and fish swimming around. It is reputed as the "West Lake of the North", and people come here from all around China to spend holidays and escape from the summer heat. The Eight Grand Views such as Diaoshuilou (Tower Hanging Waters) Waterfall, Zhenzhumen (Pearl Gate), Daxiaogushan (Big and Lesser Gushan Hills) possess many moving fairy tales and are most famous. Among them, Diaoshuilou Waterfall is one of the most well-known waterfalls in China. The 40-meter-wide waterfall has a 25 meter drop of elevation. It runs all the year round forming a spectacular view with rising spray, beautiful rainbow and deafening sound.

Daxing'anling Area: Located at the northernmost tip of China, the beautiful and richly endowed Daxing'anling (Greater Hinggan Mountains, literally, Ridge of Great Prosperousness and Peacefulness) borders on the stretching and undulating Xiaoxing'anling (Lesser Hinggan Mountains) in the east, the immense Hulun Buir Grassland in the west and the fertile Songnen Plain in the south, and faces Russia across the Heilong (Black Dragon) River in the north. In the area, mountains rising one higher than another are covered with opulent forests, which offers a vigorous and spectacular view. The Daxing'anling is the largest modernized forest zone of China with an area of 85,000 square kilometers

and a timber quantity of 5 hundred million cubic meters. It is also a natural zoo and botanical garden in circumpolar latitude area supporting more than 1,000 species of plants and 400 types of rare animals and birds including red deer, reindeer, sika deer, roe deer, wild boar, snow hare, brown bear, sable, pheasant, swan and so on. Additionally, many varieties of cold water fishes lived in the rivers and lakes crisscrossed the area. A local saying goes "A wielding of stick must result in a river deer, a scoop of water must have a fish, and a pheasant would fly into a pan itself", which vividly describes the abundant resource of wild animals there. Daxing'anling features clear-cut season, with spring flowers, summer sea of forest, autumn red leaf and winter snow highlighting each season. It is a comprehensive scenic area for sightseeing, hunting, fishing and drifting.

Wudalianchi: Situated in the city with the same name in the north of Heilongjiang Province, Wudalianchi is a famous scenic spot of China. More than 200 years ago when the volcanoes erupted continuously, the molten lava pouring down from the crater blocked a river and created a string of five smaller lakes. These five lakes, one linking the other and meandering northward, are collectively known as Wudalianchi,

which means five great connected lakes in Chinese. The scenery here is spectacular, with beautiful peaks, grotesque shaped rocks, secluded lakes and magical springs. A total of 14 cone-shaped volcanoes including Laohei (Old Black) and Huoshao (Burn) rise sheer from level ground, layer upon layer and range upon range, and plus the luxuriant vegetation and rocks of various shapes scattered among them, form an integral whole with the surrounding landscape. Additionally, Wudalianchi is also famous for the natural mineral water gushing from the mountain springs, which, containing many elements and minerals beneficial to health, have been proven to have certain curative effects for a number of diseases. Known as the "Volcanic Park" and "Natural Volcanic Geological Museum", the area attracts scientist and researchers as well as tourists.

→
吉林省长白山黑凤口
Heifengkou (Pass of Black Wind) of the Changbai Mountain, Jilin Province

河北省坝上草原
Bashang Grassland, Hebei Province

河北省承德市避暑山庄
Mountain resort, Chengde
City, Hebei Province

河北省坝上大峡谷
Bashang Grand Gorge,
Hebei Province

河北省坝上草原白杨林
White Poplar Forest on the
Bashang Grassland, Hebei Province

山西省壺口瀑布
Hukou Waterfall, Shanxi Province

1. 河北省北戴河鸽子窝
   Dove Nest at Beidaihe Beach Resort,
   Hebei Province

2. 山西省恒山风景区悬空寺
   Midair Temple in the Hengshan
   Mountain Scenic Area, Shanxi Province

3. 内蒙古自治区呼伦湖
   Lake Hulun, Inner Mongolia

3

1. 内蒙古自治区巴丹吉林沙漠
Patanchilin Desert, Inner Mongolia
Autonomous Region

2. 内蒙古自治区巴丹吉林沙漠胡杨
Diversiform-Leaved Poplar in the
Patanchilin Desert, Inner Mongolia
Autonomous Region

3. 内蒙古自治区额尔古纳河
Argun River, Inner Mongolia
Autonomous Region

4. 内蒙古自治区响沙湾景区
Resonant Sand Gorge Tourist Zone,
Inner Mongolia Autonomous Region

4

1.2.内蒙古自治区草原风光
Scenery of Grassland in Inner
Mongolia Autonomous Region

3.内蒙古自治区根河
Genhe River, Inner Mongolia
Autonomous Region

2

1. 内蒙古自治区鄂尔多斯高原
Ordos Plateau, Inner Mongolia
Autonomous Region

2. 辽宁省葫芦岛市海滨冬景
Winter Scenery of the Sea in
Huludao City, Liaoning Province

3. 辽宁省红海滩
Red Beach Resort, Liaoning
Province

3

1.辽宁省千山大佛
  Giant Buddha of Qianshan
  Mountain, Liaoning Province

2.吉林省长白山隆冬
  Changbai Mountain in Winter,
  Jilin Province

3.吉林省长白山密林
  Dense Forest on the Changbai
  Mountain, Jilin Province

吉林省长白山天池
**Tianchi Lake of the Changbai
Mountain, Jilin Province**

长白山
Changbai Mountain

长白山位于吉林省东南部、中朝两国交界处，因顶部多为白浮岩组成，且每年有8个月的积雪期，山如银盔素甲，因此得名。长白山总面积8000多平方千米，主峰白云峰海拔2749米，此外，海拔2500米以上的山峰有10余座，被誉为"关东第一名山"，与黑龙江并称为"白山黑水"，已成为中国东北的代名词。

长白山是一座休眠火山，据史料记载，近300年间曾有过3次喷发，形成了包括火山锥体、台地、火山口湖、断裂带等独特的自然奇观和绮丽迷人的景观。由于山地地形受垂直变化的影响，长白山从山脚到山顶，随着高度的增加还形成了阔叶林、针阔混交林、针叶林、岳桦林、苔原地带等景观带，植被保存完好，是我国三大自然资源宝库之一，也是世界重要的物种基因库。美丽富饶的长白山生长着2300多种植物和1100多种动物，包括东北虎、金钱豹、猞猁、马鹿、梅花鹿、麝、斑羚、黑貂、黑熊、棕熊、鸳鸯、丹顶鹤、天鹅、黑鹳等国家重点保护动物。1980年，长白山被联合国确定为国际生物圈保护区。

在长白山丰富的自然景观中，天池堪称其最。它位于白云峰山顶，是一个火山喷发自然形成的火山口湖，海拔2194米，为中朝两国的界湖。长白山天池湖泊南北长4.85千米，东西宽3.35千米，平均水深204米，最深处373米，是我国最深的湖泊。湖水常年清澈碧绿，周围群山环绕，从空中俯瞰宛如一面天外飞来的仙镜，又似镶嵌在奇峰万石之巅的一块瑰丽的碧玉。加之这里气候瞬息万变，经常云雾缭绕，天池时隐时现，使人感到神秘莫测，景色绝妙。湖周芳草茵茵，鲜花朵朵，是游人观光历险之地。天池的湖水从北面一个缺口溢出，缓流1000多米，突然奔腾咆哮，从悬崖飞泻而下，形成著名的长白山大瀑布，落差达60余米，非常壮观。它是松花江的源头，为我国东北地区海拔最高的山地型瀑布。长白瀑布附近有一个分布面积达1000平方米的温泉群，水温均在60摄氏度左右，富含多种矿物质，可治疗皮肤病、关节炎等多种疾病。长白山上还有小天池、圆池、王池等诸多火山湖。

The world-famous Changbai (Ever White) Mountain is located in the southeast of Jilin Province, bordering on D.P.R. Korea. Mainly composed of white rocks, its top is covered with snow for 8 months of a year, like wearing silver helmet, hence the name. The main peak Baiyunfeng (White Cloud Peak) rises 2,749 meters above sea level, and is surrounded by more than 10 peaks which are all over 2,500 meters in elevation. With an area of 8,000 square kilometers, the Changbai Mountain enjoys a reputation of the "First Famous Mountain in Northeast China". The word "Baishan Heishui (literally, white mountain and black water)", which refers to the Changbai Mountian and Heilong (Black Dragon) River, has become a synonym for the Northeast.

Changbai Mountain is a sleeping volcano, and its 3 eruptions occurred during the latest 300 years, which gave birth to the unique natural wonders such as volcano cones, tablelands, carter lakes and riftzones, as well as fascinating scenery. The dense forest there is the first big attraction for tourists. There's a large variety of plant species on the mountainside, different kinds of plants from the Temperate Zone and the Frigid Zone including broad-leaved forest, mingled forest broad-leaved trees and conifers, coniferous forest, Betula ermaii Cramisso forest and tundra zone. It is famed as one of the Three Treasure-Houses of Natural Resources and precious biological gene bank of the species in the world. With a well-preserved natural environment and ecosystem, it is rich in biological species characteristic of mountainous regions. Among the rare animals living in the preserve are Manchurian tiger, Panthera pardus, lynx, red deer, sika deer, musk deer, Naemorhedus goral, sable, black bear, brown bear, mandarin duck, red-crowned crane, swan and Ciconia nigra, all having been listed as rare animals under state protection. In 1980, the Changbai Mountain was list in the International Man and Biosphere Reserve Network by the UNESCO.

Endowed with rich natural resources and charming scenery, the mountains are dotted with scenic spots, of which the Tianchi (Heavenly Lake) is most famous. It lies on the top of Baiyunfeng, and straddles the China-Korea border. A natural crater lake, Tianchi is 2,194 meters above sea level. Its average depth is 204 meters, and some places reach 373 meters beneath the surface, which makes it the deepest lake in China. About 4.85 kilometers long from south to north and 3.35 kilometers from east to west, the lake is surrounded by mountain. Overlooking from the air, Tianchi with its limpid water resembles celestial's mirror falling down from the heaven, or flawless jasper inlaid into mountains. Sometimes, the lake can be so placid as to have a mirror-like surface and the reflections of the snow-capped peaks will be shimmering in the reply water. At such a beautiful sight, one will feel completely relaxed and tranquil at heart. But sometimes the lake can also present a mysterious sight when it is shrouded in clouds appearing and disappearing from time to time. The lakeside is covered throughout with a carpet of green grass and dotted with flowers. All these make Tianchi an unmatched attraction. The lake water overflows from a notch on the north bank of Tianchi, and flows slowly for about 1,000 meters. Then suddenly it pours down forming a spectacular 60-meter waterfall, which is the highest mountain waterfall in northeast China. The water ends up flowing into the Songhua River, one of the most important rivers in the north. Lying to the north of the Tianchi Lake is a large group of hot springs with an area of over 1,000 square meters. The water temperature measures higher than 60 centigrade. Thanks to the presence of many mineral salts including hydrogen sulphide, the water here has a good therapeutic effect on many kinds of disease. Now there are a number of sanatoriums to cater for the visitors. As the water contains abundant mineral substances, bathing pools have been built to provide rheumatic arthritis and dermatoses treatment. Apart from the Tianchi Lake, on the mountain are Lesser Tianchi, Yuanchi (Round Lake), Wangchi (King Lake) and other volcanic lakes.

吉林省松花江雾凇
Rimed Trees along the
Songhua River, Jilin Province

1.黑龙江省镜泊湖
Jingpo Lake, Heilongjiang Province

2.黑龙江省镜泊湖吊水楼瀑布
Diaoshuilou (Tower Hanging Waters)
Waterfall in Jingpo Lake Scenic Area,
Heilongjiang Province

3.黑龙江省五大连池
Wudalianchi, Heilongjiang Province

2

1.2.黑龙江省五大连池
Wudalianchi, Heilongjiang
Province

3.黑龙江省五大连池景区火山岩
Volcanic rock in Wudalianchi
Scenic Area, Heilongjiang
Province

黑龙江省大兴安岭
Daxing'anling, Heilongjiang Province

河北省金山岭云海
Sea of Clouds of Jinshanling
Great Wall, Hebei Province